p.74

Psychology for Church Leaders Series

# FRACTURED PERSONALITIES

## The Psychology of Mental Illness

Gary R. Collins

**CREATION HOUSE**
**CAROL STREAM, ILLINOIS**

FIRST EDITION
Library of Congress Catalog Card Number 72-189629

# ACKNOWLEDGMENTS

For permission to reprint excerpts in this book, acknowledgment is made to the following publishers:

*Christianity Today*—for excerpts from Anonymous, "Letter from a Homosexual," March 1, 1968 issue.

Wm. B. Eerdmans Publishing Company—for excerpts from E. Sauer, *In the Arena of Faith,*©1955.

Holt, Rinehart and Winston, Inc.—for excerpts from Erich Fromm, *The Sane Society,*©1955.

The Macmillan Co.—for excerpts from M. Zax and G. Stricker, *Patterns of Psychopathology,*©1963.

McGraw-Hill Book Company, Inc.—for excerpts from Benjamin B. Wolman (ed.) *Handbook of Clinical Psychology,* ©1965; George Kisker, *The Disorganized Personality,* ©1964; and Brendan A. Maher, *Principles of Psychopathology,*©1966.

W. W. Norton & Co., Inc.—for excerpts from A. M. Rose, ed. *Mental Health and Mental Disorder,*©1955.

Pan Books, Ltd.—for excerpts from William Sargant, *Battle for the Mind,* 1957.

Prentice-Hall, Inc.—for excerpts from T. L. Duncan, *Understanding and Helping the Narcotic Addict,*©1965.

W. B. Saunders Co.—for excerpts from Ephraim Rosen and Ian Gregory, *Abnormal Psychology,*©1965.

Scott, Foresman, and Co.—for excerpts from James C. Coleman, *Abnormal Psychology and Modern Life* (third edition),©1964.

John Wiley and Son, Inc.—for excerpts from A. B. Hollingshead and F. C. Redlich, *Social Class and Mental Illness,*©1958.

# CONTENTS

# PREFACE

This is the third volume in the Psychology for Church Leaders Series. In the first volume, *Man in Transition*, we looked at normal behavior and discussed some of the challenges that all of us face in our transition through life. We considered spiritual development in different age groups and suggested some ways in which psychology can assist church leaders in their ministry to people who are meeting the stresses of modern living.

But what do people do when the stresses get too great? Frequently they turn to counselors for help and, more often than not, people take their problems to a pastor or other church leader. In the second volume of this series, *Effective Counseling*, we discussed counseling techniques, considered some common counseling problems, and suggested ways in which the church can prevent new problems from developing or existing problems from getting worse.

To help people with their problems, however, we need more than an understanding of counseling skills. We also need to know something about the nature and causes of mental illness. It is for this reason that *Fractured Personalities* has been written. I have tried to survey much of the professional literature on the subject of abnormal behavior and to present a summary which is concise, accurate and relevant for the church leader who has neither the time nor training to plow through the psychological journals for himself. This book is not written as a comprehensive introduction to the field of mental illness. Instead, I have presented the psychological conclusions which, in my opinion, are the most relevant and practical for the church leader. In a very real sense, then, this is a book on "what the church

9

worker should know about abnormal behavior."

What is abnormal behavior? The prefix *ab* means "away from;" thus to be *ab*-normal is to be acting in a way that is away from or different from that which is normal.

But what is *normal*? This is a word which we frequently use but are not always able to define. Several years ago a statistician, an educator, a sociologist, an anthropologist, a philosopher, a lawyer, a psychoanalyst, a botanist, a psychiatrist, a neurologist, a theologian and a psychologist all got together to discuss what was meant by "normal behavior." As they spoke, each of these experts used the terms *normal* and *abnormal* in a little different way, and the chairman of the meeting had great difficulty in finding a definition which could be accepted by everyone.[1]

Some people will quarrel with the definition given below but in the chapters which follow, we will be using the term *abnormality* in three ways:

First, *a person is abnormal if his behavior is at odds with the social expectations of the society in which he lives.* The murderer, dope addict, sex deviate, hermit, or hebephrenic who sits by himself and giggles, are all "abnormal" because their actions differ from that which society considers to be normal.

When we think of abnormality in this way we must recognize that what is abnormal in one society may not be abnormal in another society. In the United States and Canada it is normal to be friendly, to laugh, or to appear happy, but it is abnormal to be overly suspicious of other people. In the Dobu culture of New Guinea just the opposite is true. Extreme suspicion of one's neighbors is normal, but laughter and expressions of happiness are taboo. The thoroughly maladjusted Dobu is the man who is pleasant and naturally friendly.[2]

When defined in this way, abnormality can also last for short or long periods of time and can result from a variety of causes. The hospital patient who is delirious after surgery

10

is showing abnormal behavior, but this is of relatively short duration and is probably the result of some temporary physical disorder.

Second, *a person is abnormal if he experiences internal conflicts which lead to intense and prolonged feelings of insecurity, anxiety or unhappiness.* Here is the individual who is at odds with himself. He has standards of behavior which he cannot attain, goals in life which he cannot reach, urges which he cannot suppress, or fears which he cannot overcome. He may feel insecure, inadequate, or without purpose or direction in life. He is often self-defeated and afraid of being condemned or rejected by others. Some of these people try to ignore their turmoil, some try to hide from it in order to preserve their self-esteem, and a few try—often without success—to face up to their difficulties. Many are able to keep their conflicts hidden and to show behavior which is socially appropriate, but others become so distracted by their inner tensions that they act in ways which society considers to be odd or unusual.

This internal turmoil is, to a large extent, culturally based. A child does not inherit inner tensions; he learns from those around him when to be anxious and insecure. The mother who fears thunderstorms passes this on to her children, while the businessman who is afraid of losing money or of failing in business, transmits these concerns to his son. The things which a church pastor learns to worry about may be very different from the issues which concern an African tribesman or a political dictator.

Third, *a person is abnormal if he is alienated or away from God.* Although he was made in God's image, man rebelled and was separated from his close communion with the Father. This separation is not normal. On the contrary, it is normal for man to be in fellowship with God. Because of this, a provision was made which enables any man who so desires to return to God. The person who acknowledges his sinful alienation from God, believes in the resurrection

11

of the Son of God, and invites Christ to be Lord of his life, returns to a state of oneness with God (Ro. 10:9). This is normal. It is a truth which applies to all men, regardless of the society in which one lives.

By defining abnormality in these three ways we are suggesting that normality is very rare indeed. In order to be completely normal one must be at peace with his society, at peace with himself, and at peace with God.

In the chapters which follow, we consider abnormality in greater detail. Beginning with a discussion of the causes of abnormal behavior, we then look at the symptoms of abnormality and the ways in which so-called "mental illness" is commonly classified, "diagnosed," and treated. The last two chapters describe some of the more common types of abnormality.

As this third volume goes to press, I continue to be grateful to the many people who have in some way helped with the production of the manuscript. Most of them have been mentioned before: my wife Julie, my colleagues and students at Trinity Evangelical Divinity School, my typist, and the men at Creation House. As I have worked on this book, I have also been much aware of the thousands of pastors and other church leaders who are in daily contact with people such as those described in the following pages. If these church workers can better understand and help the fractured personalities in their midst, if the families of distressed people can become more sympathetic and tolerant, and if people under pressure can read this book and better appreciate their own reactions to stress, then my labors in producing this manuscript will not have been in vain.

GARY R. COLLINS

# 1

## Causes of Abnormal Behavior

Mike—that's not his real name—was twenty years old when he first arrived at the mental hospital accompanied by his pastor. As we talked, he squirmed in his chair, complained of tension, made a number of loud demands, and volunteered that he was thinking of killing himself because he couldn't stand the pain in his head. The pastor has tried to help Mike to "get a hold of himself" but since they didn't seem to be making any progress they had come to the hospital for professional assistance.

Mike had attended church all of his life and was clearly a Christian. His parents had pretty much ignored him, however, except to point out his faults, and the home had been characterized by almost constant arguing and bickering. Mike was a good-looking young man who wanted to be a physical-education teacher but his parents didn't give him any encouragement. On his own he went to college, successfully completed his first year, and became engaged to a girl who finally gave him the attention and love that he had never had at home.

Then at the end of his freshman year Mike came down with mononucleosis, his girl broke the engagement, and his parents announced that they had filed for a divorce. Suddenly Mike's disposition changed. Instead of the pleasant, friendly person whom everyone liked, he became cranky, complaining about everything, depressed, and worrying about all kinds of physical symptoms. He was fired from his summer job and in a rage he attempted to castrate his father.

13

A lot of people are fascinated and somewhat awe-struck by the actions of emotionally disturbed people. Why, we wonder, would anyone with as much potential as Mike suddenly become bitter and depressed? Why do people jump from tall buildings, develop sexual perversions, or reach the irrational conclusion that they are always being spied upon? To answer these questions we must start with a consideration of why people become mentally ill and fragmented personalities in the first place.

There is a tendency among Christians to assume that all abnormal behavior is caused by some spiritual problem. Certainly it is true that emotional break-downs often do result from one's spiritual condition, but to suggest this as the only explanation is a gross oversimplification. Every year, psychologists, psychiatrists and other professionals devote long hours to research and careful debate aimed at finding the precise reasons for abnormality. The conclusion reached by almost all of these researchers is that the causes of abnormal behavior are varied and extremely complex.

This complexity might be illustrated by reference to the old saying about "the straw that breaks the camel's back." The "break" in this situation can be attributed to two conditions. First, there is the weight of the straw. Since this precipitates or brings about a break in the animal's back, the straw could be called a *precipitating* stress. But the effect of this stress largely depends on the strength of the *predisposing* factors. They describe the state of the animal at the time of stress and provide an explanation for the' animal's ability to bear any additional pressure.

The left-hand column in Figure 1-1 summarizes the causes of abnormality and shows how precipitating and predisposing factors can work together to bring about a change in the efficient functioning of an individual. It should be noted that there are numerous factors, both within the individual and within the environment, which can operate simultaneously to influence behavior.

14

## PRECIPITATING FACTORS
### (Stress)

#### Biological Precipitating Stress

1. Biological deprivation
   — sleep deprivation
   — nutritional deprivation
2. Disease or infections
3. Brain damage
4. Drugs and other chemical agents

#### Psychological Precipitating Stress

#### Sociological Precipitating Stress

1. War
2. Civilian catastrophe
3. Accidents
4. Occupational and economic trends
5. Marriage
6. Technological change

#### Spiritual Precipitating Stress

1. Sin
2. Guilt
3. Tensions within the church

## PREDISPOSING FACTORS
### (State of the individual at the time of stress)

#### Biological Predisposing Factors

1. Heredity
2. Constitution
3. Glandular dysfunction
4. Congenital and acquired defects
5. Other physical factors

#### Psychological Predisposing Factors

1. Early upbringing
   — maternal deprivation and neglect
   — rejection
   — parental overprotection
   — parental overindulgence and permissiveness
   — rigid, perfectionistic demands
2. Early family disharmony
3. Early trauma
4. Inadequate learning
5. Individual differences in perception

#### Sociological Predisposing Factors

1. Occupation
2. Social class
3. Cultural group
4. Place of residence
5. Minority group membership
6. Sex
7. Marital status
8. Religious affiliation

#### Spiritual Predisposing Factors

1. Lack of meaning to life
2. Lack of belief in Christ
3. Fear

## ACTING SINGLY OR IN COMBINATION TO PRODUCE. . .

## CHANGES IN THE ORGANISM

1. Changes in perception.
2. Changes in psysiological, psychological, sociological and/or spiritual functioning.

SHOWN IN . . .

DETECTED BY . . .

## SIGNS AND SYMPTOMS
### (Clinical manifestations)

#### Physical Symptoms

#### Psychological behavior changes

1. Attack, withdrawal or compromise
3. Use of defensive mechanisms
3. Psychological behavior such as
   — faulty perception
   — distorted thinking
   — faulty emotional expression
   — unusual motor activity
   — disorientation
   — other odd behavior

#### Social movements

#### Spiritual signs

1. Prolonged guilt feelings
2. Prolonged incapacitating doubt
3. Fanatacism

## ASSESSMENT
### (Tests and detection techniques)

#### Physiological Diagnostic Procedures

1. X-ray
2. EEG
3. Urinalysis
4. Blood pressure
5. Blood chemistry, etc.

#### Psychological Assessment Techniques

1. Interviews
2. Psychological Tests
   — systematic observation
   — self-respect techniques
   — performance tests

#### Sociological Assessment Techniques

1. Interviews
2. Questionnaires
3. Observation, etc.

#### Spiritual Assessment

1. Interviews
2. Observation, etc.

---

### Figure 1-1

## Causes, Symptoms and Assessment of Abnormal Behavior

Adapted from Guze, Matarazzo and Saslow (1953);

Collins (1969); and Coleman and Broen (1972).

## Precipitating Factors

The human nervous system is perpetually bombarded with a wide variety of sounds, sights, thoughts, feelings and other stimuli, most of which are received without the organism's ever becoming consciously aware of their existence. The ticking of a clock, the noise in the street outside, the pressure of clothes against the skin, or the chest movements that accompany breathing are all examples of stimulations which we rarely even notice. Other stimulations—such as the ringing of a telephone, feelings of midday hunger, of the change of a traffic light from red to green—influence people at a conscious level, but most of us are able to respond quickly and with relative ease. Some consciously perceived stimulations—like a gnawing headache or a constantly ringing telephone—cause us to feel sick, annoyed or irritated; but even when faced with frustrating situations such as these, most people can, with effort, make an adequate response or adjustment.

Still other stimulations, however, make far greater demands on the individual. The threatened breakup of a marriage, the sudden death of a family member, the realization that one has a serious illness, the failure to pass an important college course, the destruction of one's property—these are situations which cannot be ignored or quickly handled. Psychologists often refer to these as *stress* situations.

Broadly defined, stress refers to any stimulation which puts pressure on a person and requires him to make difficult adjustments. Sometimes this stress is so excessive that the individual is not able to adjust well, if at all. His resources are overtaxed, his behavior ceases to be efficient or organized, and he may respond with a variety of behavior abnormalities. This is what happened to Mike as he experienced a number of stresses which came in rapid succession.

At times a single stress can bring about a breakdown in behavior. In other cases several precipitating stresses must combine before behavior abnormalities appear. Sometimes

16

it is easy to identify the stress or stresses which precipitate a breakdown, but often such identification is very difficult. For purposes of discussion we give separate consideration to biological, psychological, sociological and spiritual stresses, but it must be remembered that in reality these all work together to influence the individual.

## BIOLOGICAL PRECIPITATING STRESS

*Biological deprivation.* Most of us are easily discouraged and unable to function efficiently when we are exceptionally tired or hungry. Occasionally such physical deprivations become extreme, and this sometimes leads to abnormal behavior.

During the Korean War, for example, *sleep deprivation* was one of the techniques used by the Communist Chinese to impair the thinking of captured prisoners and extract untrue "confessions." More recently several experimenters have studied sleep deprivation in detail by depriving people of sleep and observing their reactions. Increased irritability, slowed reaction time, confused thinking, memory lapses, hallucinations, and other abnormal reactions have all been observed.[1] Several years ago, two radio announcers staged a contest to determine who could stay awake for the longer period of time. In the 168½ hours during which the contestants went without sleep (at that time the attending physician terminated the contest and declared it a tie), many signs of abnormality were observed, some of which persisted for weeks after the contest. The behavior of one contestant was particularly dramatic:

> His close friends observed a marked change in his personality after the marathon. He told conflicting stories about his past and seemed overwhelmed when confronted by the discrepancies. His thinking developed a bizarre flavor. He developed the delusion that he was responsible for the Egyptian-Israeli conflict and that a female secret agent in Florida was trying to get him to return to the Suez Canal zone. He used poor judgment in the management of personal and financial affairs. He was irritable in his work, and often

17

failed to show up at all. He was troubled by insomnia at night and lapses of attention and memory during the day. Finally, the patient's affairs became so confused that he sought hospitalization.[2]

Several studies have shown that *nutritional deprivation* can also lead to behavior abnormalities. During the Second World War, a group of conscientious objectors volunteered to participate in a study of semi-starvation. Normal calorie intake was reduced by about 50 percent, and the men lived on this reduced diet for six months. The men lost about one-fourth of their previous body weight, but the changes in behavior were even more dramatic. They became depressed, irritable, apathetic, and unable to sleep. They lost their sense of humor, became disinterested in other people, and thought about food perpetually. When they were tested with the Minnesota Multiphasic Personality Inventory (a psychological test which is used to identify various kinds of psychiatric conditions), their answers were neurotic.[3] Other studies have shown that a lack of sugar, vitamin deficiencies, and reduced amounts of iodine, calcium or salt in the diet can all influence human behavior.

*Disease and infections.* People who are ill frequently show behavior which is abnormal. Experimenters such as Janis, whose work with surgery patients was described in *Man in Transition*, have shown that the physical and psychological stress associated with an operation can lead to confusion, apprehension, fear, depression, anger and resentment.[4] In addition, diseases such as malaria, influenza, pneumonia, smallpox, scarlet fever, or typhoid fever can be accompanied by personality changes and by restless, irritable, dazed, confused or delirious behavior.[5] Usually as the patient improves physically the abnormal behavior symptoms also disappear, although in some cases a more prolonged behavior abnormality results. This is especially likely when the central nervous system has been affected in some way.

Probably syphilis (which is currently on the rise in our society) is the clearest example of an infection which causes abnormal behavior. During the act of sexual intercourse an infected individual transmits a microscopic organism to his or her partner. Shortly thereafter a hard pimple or open sore appears in the genital area, accompanied by a rash and sometimes by headaches or fever. If treated at this time the disease can be stopped, but if untreated the symptoms disappear and the disease persists even though there is no outward indication of its presence. Slowly the central nervous system is destroyed, the blood vessels are unable to function properly, and the brain is literally eaten away. This condition leads to a number of psychological abnormalities such as poor judgment, disorientation, loss of memory, delusions, and bizzare irrational actions.

*Brain damage.* Damage to the brain, with resulting behavioral abnormalities, occurs in ways other than through infections such as syphilis. A sudden deprivation of oxygen, the introduction of harmful chemicals into the bloodstream, the development of a tumor with resulting pressure on the brain, a stroke (which is the blockage of an artery with a consequent reduction in the blood supply to the brain), or a severe blow on the head, can all produce brain damage. Popular expressions such as "he must have been dropped on his head when he was a baby" indicate a widely held and scientifically verified belief that brain injury can cause abnormal behavior. It should be noted, however, that portions of an adult brain can be damaged or removed with little noticeable change in behavior. In his study of brain-injured war veterans, Goldstein reported that following a brief period of behavior disorganization, such patients were still able to function with good efficiency. [6]

*Drugs and other chemical agents.* Drugs such as bromides, barbituates, sulfa, morphine and cocaine; toxic agents such as large doses of X-ray or lead poisoning (sometimes acquired by swallowing paint or breathing its fumes); or the inhalation of carbon monoxide and other gases, can all lead to behavioral malfunctioning. This is due usually to the influence of these substances on the central nervous system.

## PSYCHOLOGICAL PRECIPITATING STRESS

Psychological stresses—such as frustrations that hinder our progress toward some goal, disruptive conflicts, and pressures—are common in each of our lives. While most of these stressful situations can be handled efficiently, some are so strong that normal defensive reactions do not work.* The individual discovers that he must use more extreme defensive techniques and, in so doing, he begins to show the exaggerated and inappropriate behavior which we know as abnormality. His attacks against what he sees as the source of stress may become violent. His withdrawal from the situation may take him to an unreal but secure little "world of his own." Defensive reactions may be clung to with unreasonable tenacity, as when rationalizations are defended in spite of mounting evidence to the contrary, or the mechanism of projection is taken to such extremes that the individual is highly suspicious of other people.

## SOCIOLOGICAL PRECIPITATING STRESS

In November, 1963, millions of people were stunned by the assassination of President John F. Kennedy. When the news reached the student body of a West Coast college where the author was at that time employed in the psychological counseling center, several students fainted and at least two students were hospitalized for several days in response to the shock of knowing that the President was dead. Kennedy's death was an international incident, but it brought stress to the lives of individuals, many of whom had never even seen the President.

*Defensive reactions are devices that our minds use to hide from stress or to help us to face stress. These are discussed in the last chapter of *Man in Transition*. Because this earlier book considered psychological stress in detail, the discussion on this page is limited to one brief paragraph.

When we use the term *sociological stress*, we are referring to those stresses which come about because of our membership in some group. The group can be small or large. A husband and wife, for example, can be thought of as a small social group. If there is friction between the members of this marital group, either or both of the people involved may experience a stress which has social origins. On a much larger scale, the term *Americans* also refers to a social group. If the country is at war or in an economic slump, individual Americans can likewise experience a stress with social origins. The family of which we are members, the church where we serve, the community where we live, the school where we study or teach, the denomination to which we belong—all of these are groups which can be a source of stress in our lives.

Sociological stress arises from at least three sources. First, there may be *friction within the group* which is stressful to the individual group members. When a church or denomination splits over some theological question, or when a family cannot agree on the choice of a vacation area, the involved individuals are likely to experience stress. Second, individual stress may arise when *one's group is in conflict with some other group or situation*. When soldiers meet the enemy, when members of opposing teams meet on the football field, or when blacks encounter whites in racially troubled areas, stress is sure to be present. Sometimes instead of groups of people in conflict with other groups, we have people united in a struggle with nature. This occurs when men fight forest fires or when volunteers pile sandbags along the banks of a rampaging river. Third, the *individual group members may be at odds with others in the group to which he belongs*. The teenager who disagrees with his local church, the political candidate who cannot accept the party platform, and the student who refuses to abide by the rules of the university administration, are all behaving in a manner which is likely to result in some sociological stress

21

within the individual and/or within the conforming members of the group.

There are at least six classes of sociological stress: war, civilian catastrophe, accidents, occupational and economic trends, marriage and family stress, and technological change. While each of these is considered here as a precipitator of abnormality, each could also be a predisposing cause of deviant behavior. War, for example, can precipitate or cause tension within the individual, but it can also lower his resistance to other pressures. When this happens, war is a predisposing factor.

*War.* War and the threat of war bring intense stress to the combatants and their families. Frequently there are forced and prolonged separation from loved ones, disruption from the routines of peacetime civilian living, threat of physical harm or death, loss of property, and economic upheaval.

How an individual will react to the stress of war depends somewhat on whether he is on the winning or losing side, and whether he is a civilian or a combatant. It has been observed that, in comparison to the losers, people who are on the winning side show more cheerfulness and a greater ability to tolerate the hardships and setbacks of the war. [7] When civilians and military men were studied in England during World War II, it was seen that the civilian populations showed a decrease of abnormality while the number of psychiatric casualities in the armed forces increased significantly. The civilians who remained at home joined with their neighbors behind a single purpose, social barriers broke down, life took on a new meaning, and personal problems faded to insignificance. In the military, however, many men experienced stressful conflict between the desire to remain alive and the desire to be good soldiers. Intense fatigue, the constant observation of death and destruction, perpetual danger, and concern about one's family at home all conflicted with the desire to demonstrate the fearless, loyal and cool behavior which is supposed to characterize

22

a devoted soldier. These conflicts, along with the anxiety that accompanies combat, can be the stress that pushes a military man past his breaking point. Such anxieties sometimes persist long after the individual has left the service and returned to civilian life.

*Civilian catastrophe.* Behavior disorders sometimes appear following earthquakes, floods, tornados, plane crashes, fires, explosions or other terrifying experiences. When involved in situations such as these, individuals frequently react with severe shock sometimes accompanied by panic. How people react to the stress of civilian catastrophe is discussed further in chapter 4.

*Accidents.* According to the World Almanac, approximately 115,000 Americans are killed annually in accidents. [8] Of these, about 55,000 die in automobile accidents, 29,000 are killed in home accidents, and 14,000 die in accidents at work. For every one person killed, approximately 95 are injured. Such accidents are highly stressful. They bring pain, disability, death, and financial crises which can precipitate abnormal behavior within both the victim and in his loved ones.

*Occupational and economic trends.* Whenever an individual experiences a financial setback, fails in business, is fired, or "laid off" from his job, he is likely to respond with despair, discouragement, and loss of self-esteem. Following the stock market crash of 1929, for example, there was a sharp rise in the number of suicides in the United States. While relatively few people kill themselves during periods of economic pressure and widespread unemployment today, occupational and economic trends often do lead to anxiety and other symptoms of behavior abnormality.

*Marriage and family stress.* At some time most church leaders have opportunity to observe the stress that comes with divorce or family problems. Two researchers once reported a study in which 500 delinquent boys were compared with 500 nondelinquents. [9] The two groups were

23

matched for age, intelligence, national origin, and location of residence in the neighborhood. It was found that 60 percent of the delinquents came from homes that had been broken by parental separation, divorce or death, while only 34 percent of the nondelinquents experienced a similar loss of parents.

Marriage breakups are not the only source of stress within a family, however. The death or sudden illness of a family member can be very traumatic, as can the arrest of a close relative, the illegitimate pregnancy of a teenage daughter, or the rebellion of a college-age son who decides to throw over the "bigoted" values and religious beliefs of his parents.

*Technological change.* If all of the world's scientists throughout the ages of history were suddenly brought back to life, they would be greatly outnumbered by the scientists who are living and working in our day. The knowledge which these men and women have discovered has produced a rapidity of technical change which is unmatched by any other period of history. With the benefits of technical development, however, there has come a swift change in moral values and behavior standards. New political ideologies have arisen. Educational methods have been revolutionized. Even theology has experienced such a cataclysmic alteration that in spite of the "Jesus people," God is still considered to be dead in some circles, and Christianity is relegated to a bygone era. According to John W. Gardner, we have been startled in recent years "by instances of runaway growth, of expansion so rapid that it outruns all control. Faced with such instances, even the most forward-looking man may be forgiven for thinking: 'This is change gone wild. This is growth so destructive of other values as to be cancerous!'" [10] Little wonder that many people are stunned by the rapid change. [11]

Many years ago it was discovered that neurosis is more prevalent in complex fast-changing communities than in

24

more static communities.[12] With the advance of technology the traditional values, loyalties and ideals of a society give the appearance of being static and "outdated." For many people who live in this changing world and must make decisions concerning the future, the old values are being thrown out with the hope that they will be replaced with something new. But new values are not easily found and, as a result, many people are floundering and groping about in search of values which will enable them to live satisfying, meaningful lives. Along with its many benefits, therefore, technological change brings an increase in anxiety, insecurity and confusion.[13]

## SPIRITUAL PRECIPITATING FACTORS

Psychologists in general tend to be critical of religion. Having observed the distorted religious beliefs that characterize many mental patients, many psychologists and psychiatrists often conclude that religion is bad; and that it is a childish wish for a "big brother in the sky" or a weak crutch for emotionally unstable people. God, prayer, worship, conversion and miracles have all been "explained" in terms of science or cast aside as issues that are of no relevance to psychology. The fact remains, however, that one's religious beliefs, spiritual condition, and association with other believers (or nonbelievers) can bring about considerable stress. Instead of denying or ignoring spiritual precipitating factors, therefore, we must try to understand how they contribute to the development of psychological abnormality.

*Sin.* The term *sin* can have two different shades of meaning. As commonly used, sin is a thought or act which goes against the rules of society or against one's own moral standards. The individual who steals, lies, or engages in sexual behavior which he believes to be wrong is engaging in the act of sin. Since this use of the term implies overt action (or thoughts about action), it might be referred to as the *sin of doing.*

25

*Sin* can also describe the state of an individual. This is the idea of original sin as expressed in such Scripture verses as Isaiah 64:6; Romans 3:10 and 3:23. This is a *sin of being*. Man *is* (sin of being) a sinner by nature, and his *actions* (sin of doing) are an outgrowth of his human nature. The sin of doing is based partly on one's culture; that is, what is right or wrong behavior depends somewhat upon the society in which one lives. The sin of being is not based on culture. "All have sinned" and "there is none righteous," regardless of the society into which one is born.

Some psychologists are now coming to realize that sins of doing can be sources of real stress. When we use the term "mental illness," suggests Dr. O. H. Mowrer,[14] we are trying to convince ourselves that disturbed people bear no responsibility for their condition.* But this is not always so. Much abnormality results because a person has violated a social regulation or personal standard, that is, because he has engaged in some act of sin. One does not have to work very long in a mental hospital before encountering some person who believes he has committed the "unpardonable" sin. Such preoccupation with sins of doing can be both a symptom and a precipitating cause of maladjustment.

While psychologists like Mowrer recognize the importance of sins of doing, they reject the idea that sins of being can have any bearing on one's emotional stability. Mowrer says the doctrine of original sin is "nonsense" and has done "much harm in the world."

Let us suppose, however, that an individual is physically healthy, able to function efficiently within his society, has

*The same idea has been suggested succinctly by a psychiatrist, Dr. Thomas S. Szasz, who believes that "mental illness is a myth, whose function it is to disguise and thus render more palatable the bitter pill of moral conflicts in human relationships ("The Myth of Mental Illness," *American Psychologist* 15 [ 1960] : 118). The reader may notice that the term "mental illness" is rarely used in this book. Terms like "psychological abnormality," "behavior disorder," "psychological maladjustment" or "abnormal behavior" seem to be more accurate.

26

productive and enjoyable work, and experiences satisfaction of his physical, social and sexual needs, and is not bothered by feelings of anxiety or insecurity. Most of us would agree that this person is well-adjusted. He may never see a psychologist or enter a mental hospital, but is he really well balanced if he is alienated from God and rebelling against Him (Ro. 6:23; Jn. 3:16)? Surely one cannot be classified as "psychologically healthy" until he acknowledges Jesus Christ as both Savior and Lord, and invites Christ to come into his life (Jn. 1:12; Rev. 3:20).

*Guilt.* Guilt has been defined as the "realization that one has violated ethical or moral or religious principles, together with a regretful feeling of lessened personal worth on that account."[15] It is a form of self-blame which is present to some degree in all of us, and which is the direct result of sin. It can function both as a predisposing factor which lowers our ability to withstand other pressures and as a potentially dangerous and destructive precipitating stress.

Just as we have divided sin into two types—sin of doing and sin of being—so we can identify two corresponding types of guilt—the guilt of doing and the guilt of being.* The *guilt of doing* is a feeling of remorse which arises because we have done something to hurt another person or alienate us from others. This was seen in Shakespeare's *Macbeth*, where both of the murderers suffered intense guilt reactions after the death of King Duncan. Macbeth responded with hallucinations while Lady Macbeth began sleepwalking and a compulsive wringing of her hands. When he sentenced Jesus to death, Pilate probably experienced this kind of guilt and then washed his hands in an apparent attempt to disassociate himself from the crucifixion.

*The guilt of doing could be roughly equated with Tournier's concept of "false guilt" and the guilt of being could be equated with "true guilt." I hesitate to use Tournier's term, however, lest the reader who is unfamiliar with the writings of Tournier get the idea that false guilt is somehow imaginary and not as influential as true guilt. It is quite possible that "false guilt" may serve as a greater precipatory stress than "true guilt."

But one need not look to literature or history to see such evidences of guilt. The boy who goes swimming and leaves the lawn unmown, the Sunday school teacher who neglects to prepare his lesson, the driver who steps on the gas in order to get through a yellow light, the pastor who "puts off" making a call to some complaining shut-in—these are everyday examples of situations which can produce the guilt of doing.

There are broad individual differences in the extent to which one is bothered by such guilt. Some people can murder and apparently feel no guilt. Others feel guilty about ignoring a "Keep off the Grass" sign and walking across the lawn. Some people hide their guilt or try to ignore it. Others attempt to make restitution. Kisker tells of a man in Minneapolis who sent the following note to the Great Northern Railway:

> GENTLEMEN:
>
> Many years ago when a youngster of high school age, I stole a ride of about two hundred miles on a box car of one of your trains. A few years later I rode your coach train one station further than my ticket called for. This has troubled my conscience all these years (47 of them). Here is payment for the rides with six percent compound interest, and asking to be forgiven for the long delay. 16

The original ticket had cost five dollars, but the man enclosed a check for $110.

Such guilt feelings can prey on an individual's mind and bring about a breakdown. Hospital patients frequently complain of their guilt and sometimes the guilty individual attempts to "punish" himself by self-torture or suicide. Mowrer believes that "in so-called mental illness or psychopathology the central problem *is* guilt, unconfessed and unatoned *real guilt.* . . .Increasingly it appears that the central fact in personality disorder is *real* guilt and that it can be radically resolved only by confession that has at least a quasi-public character." 17

28

Whereas the guilt of doing is widely recognized by psychologists, the *guilt of being* is largely ignored. This is a feeling of remorse which comes from the realization that one is disobedient and at odds with the will of God. The Holy Spirit apparently exposes us to this guilt through Scripture (2 Ti. 3:16), through the words of Spirit-controlled men (Ac. 4:31), or through some unexplainable inner voice (Ro. 1:18-19). A realization that one is alienated from God can be a source of intense stress which can lead to a number of symptoms of abnormality.

*Tension within the church.* Strife between disagreeing factions is always stressful for the participants, whether the strife is within the church or without. When a church splits, however, and both sides claim to be "following the will of God," the tension is particularly acute and could precipitate a breakdown.

## PREDISPOSING FACTORS

At 11:40 p.m. on April 14, 1912, the "unsinkable" liner *Titanic* struck an iceberg in the north Atlantic and began to go down. Two hours and forty minutes later, the "largest and most glamorous ship in the world" slipped quietly beneath the cold glassy sea and carried approximately fifteen hundred people to a watery grave. In his vivid description of the *Titanic's* last night, Walter Lord describes the different responses of the people who were facing the "supreme crisis of their lives."[18] Even when they realized that the ship was sinking and that all were faced with the prospect of imminent death, those on board showed a variety of reactions. Prior to this time, each person on the ship had been influenced by a different set of biological, psychological, sociological and spiritual experiences. These different predisposing factors apparently governed the way in which each of the passengers and crewmen reacted to the stress of possible death in the freezing Atlantic.

As with the precipitating stresses, it is difficult if not impossible to identify and separate the predisposing factors

29

that determine how a given person will react to stress. Some past events may influence behavior more than others. A serious illness in childhood, the divorce of one's parents, or a conversion experience, for example, could have considerable effect on one's ability to tolerate frustration at some later time in life. More often, the biological, psychological, sociological and spiritual predispositions which are discussed separately below exert a combined influence on the individual.

### BIOLOGICAL PREDISPOSING FACTORS

*Heredity.* Whenever a patient enters a mental hospital, his or her relatives are likely to wonder at some time if mental disturbances are inherited. One of the ways in which this question can be investigated is to make a study of identical and fraternal twins. *Identical* twins have exactly the same heredity. Following the fertilization of the egg by the sperm, the fertilized egg splits and two individuals develop. In contrast, *fraternal* twins are born at the same time but do not have the same heredity. The fraternal twins develop from two different eggs which are produced simultaneously in the mother's womb and are fertilized independently by two different sperm cells. Twins are born once in every 98 American births, but only about 37 percent of these twins are identical.

If one twin shows some abnormality in behavior, what is the likelihood of the other twin showing the same abnormality? Table 1-1 summarizes the work of Kallman and others who have studied thousands of pairs of twins. The average person has less than one chance in 100 of ever becoming schizophrenic (.9 percent). If a fraternal twin is schizophrenic, however, the other twin's chances of developing schizophrenia raise to 14.5 in 100. With identical twins the odds rise sharply. When one identical twin develops schizophrenia, there are 86.2 chances in 100 that the other twin will develop the same disorder.

Since identical twins have the same heredity, the findings

reported in Table 1-1 would seem to indicate that hereditary influences are a major cause of abnormality. The fact that behavior disorders tend to run in families might seem to support his conclusion.

*Table 1-1*

**Likelihood of developing abnormality in nonrelatives, fraternal twins, and identical twins.***

| Psychiatric Condition | Percent who develop the disorder | | |
|---|---|---|---|
| | General Population | Fraternal Twins (two eggs) | Identical Twins (one egg) |
| Schizophrenia | .9 | 14.5 | 86.2 |
| Childhood Schizophrenia | | 17.1 | 70.6 |
| Neurosis and Psychopathic Personality | .4 | 26.3 | 95.7 |
| Involutional Psychosis | 1.0 | 6.0 | 60.0 |
| Adult Male Homosexuality | | 42.3 | 100.0 |

Unfortunately, the answer is not that simple. Other studies of identical twins raised in different homes have shown marked differences between the pairs, and this must be due to environmental influences. It may be, therefore, that family trends in the development of abnormality might be due more to environmental similarities than to inheritance.

In spite of recent advances in the field of human genetics there is still much debate concerning the extent to which behavior abnormalities are inherited.[19] In our present state

*Adapted from L. A. Hurst "Genetic Factors" in *Handbook of Clinical Psychology,* ed. B. B. Wolman, pp. 160-61.

of knowledge, however, at least three conclusions seem justified.

First, it is clear that heredity and environment both contribute to the development of behavior abnormalities. If an individual is mentally ill, this does not necessarily mean that his relatives will also be disturbed. Two reasons support this conclusion. First, the relatives may never encounter sufficiently strong precipitating stress, and second, each person's unique ability to tolerate stress is due to a combination of both inborn and learned factors. There is a tendency for psychopathology to run in families, but clearly this is due to similarities both in heredity *and* in environmental experiences.

Second, it is highly unlikely that one ever inherits a specific disorder such as schizophrenia or manic-depressive psychosis. It is more reasonable to assume that one inherits a predisposition or likelihood to develop a behavior abnormality. Perhaps some people are born with characteristics that lower their later stress-tolerance level.

Third, there is no necessary connection between heredity and curability. A predisposition to develop tuberculosis, for example, is known to be inherited, but the disease is nevertheless curable and preventable.[20] Likewise with behavior abnormalities; lasting recoveries are still possible and common, even in persons who have a long family history of psychopathology.

In counseling with the relatives of mental-hospital patients, the Christian leader can discuss these conclusions; but with knowledge of genetics changing so rapidly, it might be wise to check periodically with local libraries or professional counselors in order to determine the most recent advances in this field.

*Constitution.* This term refers to the enduring biological characteristics of an individual. It includes the physical features that one has inherited plus environmental modifications of these features. Physique, sex, color of skin, facial features, temperament and intelligence, for example, are all inherited, but can be modified by environmental influences.

From the time of Hippocrates, men have observed that persons with similar biological characteristics also show similar psychological traits. The person who is short and fat, like Santa Claus, is expected to be jovial and good-humored. The tall, thin individual is assumed to be a thinker. This idea has been expressed in a Greek proverb, "A gross belly does not produce a refined mind"; an old English expression, "Fat and merry, lean and sad"; and a famous quotation from Shakespeare, "Let me have men about me that are fat . . . Yond Cassius has a lean and hungry look; he thinks too much: such men are dangerous." Some writers have suggested that the amount of stress which one can tolerate will depend to some extent to one's constitution.

Dr. William Sheldon of Harvard University is one of numerous researchers who have attempted to study this problem scientifically. Sheldon obtained physical measurements from several thousand people and concluded that the population could be divided into about eighty-eight physical categories which he called *"somatotypes."* He then attempted to determine if there was a correlation between physical type and psychiatric diagnosis. In a study of 3,000 schizophrenics and 300 manic-depressives, Sheldon found little consistent relationship between body build and psychopathology.

Work in this fascinating field is continuing on both sides of the Atlantic, but at present there is no clear-cut evidence to suggest that constitution alone is a predisposing factor in the development of behavior abnormalities.

*Glandular disfunction.* When the glands are not working properly there may be abnormalities in growth, sexual development, or activity level. Frequently such physical malfunctioning is accompanied by behavior abnormalities and a lowered resistance to stress.

*Congenital and acquired defects.* Each year in the United States and Canada several thousand infants are born with some kind of physical or mental defect. Add to this the number of people who have acquired permanent defects or long-term incapacitation because of falls, accidents, war, freak weather conditions (such as tornados or earthquakes), or chronic diseases, and it is discovered that hundreds of thousands of Americans and Canadians are handicapped in some way. These defects include such diverse symptoms as blindness, paralysis, heart disease, brain injury, degenerative diseases, mental retardation and physical deformities.

Physical defects can be the source of considerable stress and discouragement, and there is evidence that disabled persons show a greater amount of abnormality than do physically normal people. However, the extent to which a defect will lower an individual's resistance to stress depends largely on the attitude of the victim and his associates. In one study it was found that people who complained about poor health were greater mental-health risks than people who said nothing or indicated that their health was good. [21] It may be, therefore, that the attitude toward one's defect or physical health is of greater importance than the actual physical state itself.

The handicapped child who is overprotected or neglected by his parents, the disabled veteran who becomes bitter and hypercritical, the heart victim who develops anxiety and self-pity—all have a greater predispostion to abnormality than does the victim who acknowledges his deformity but seeks to rise above it. Of course the patient understanding and encouragement of relatives and church members greatly helps to alter the outlook of the handicapped person and his relatives. Some of the world's greatest contributions have been made by people who have risen above their defects. Beethoven, who continued to write music in spite of his hearing loss, is an example. So is the apostle Paul,

34

who continued to serve in spite of a physical defect (2 Co. 12:7-10).

*Other physical factors.* The influences of inherited and constitutional characteristics, glandular malfunctioning, and congential or acquired defects, are not the only factors which can lower one's resistance to stress. Sleep deprivation, nutritional deprivation, and the influence of chemical agents have been discussed as precipitating biological factors, but each of these can wear down the body and bring a greater biological predisposition to abnormality. In the case of Mike, whom we discussed at the beginning of the chapter, the mononucleosis undoubtedly lowered his ability to handle the stresses of his parents' divorce and his own engagement coming to an end.

## PSYCHOLOGICAL PREDISPOSING FACTORS

*Early upbringing.* In working with his patients, Freud noted that a child's experiences during the first few years of life seem to have an influence on adult behavior. This observation led Freud and his followers to study early experience and subsequently a number of non-Freudian psychologists became interested in testing the poet's assumption that the "child is father to the man."

Maternal deprivation and neglect, rejection, parental overprotection, overindulgence, permissiveness, and rigid perfectionistic demands have all been shown to adversely influence childhood adjustment and have an unhealthy influence on subsequent adult behavior.

1. Maternal deprivation and neglect. In the thirteenth century, a historian named Salimbene described the attempt of a King Frederick II to raise children without maternal affection:

> He wanted to find out what kind of speech and what manner of speech children would have when they grew up if they spoke to no one beforehand. So he bade foster mothers and nurses to suckle the children, to bathe and wash them but in no way to prattle with them, or to speak to them, for

35

he wanted to learn whether they would speak the Hebrew language, which was the oldest, or Greek, or Latin, or Arabic, or perhaps the language of their parents, of whom they had been born. But he labored in vain because the children all died. For they could not live without the petting and joyful faces and loving words of their foster mothers.

More recent research by psychologists has shown that the child who is neglected in early life and deprived of close contact with a mother is likely to feel frustrated, insecure and tense. Often the development of these children is slow and when they reach adulthood they continue to be anxious, insecure, and sometimes hostile. In such cases their ability to tolerate stress is lowered because of their upbringing.

2. Rejection. Sometimes parents supply the material needs of their children but intentionally or unintentionally withhold love. Parents who reject their children often emphasize shortcomings, are overly severe in their punishment, make unfavorable comparisons with other children, and sometimes state deliberately that the child is unwanted. Children soon perceive this rejection and develop the idea that they are worthless and insignificant. Certainly if the parents convey the impression that he is "no good," it is difficult for the child to view himself in a positive way.

While such children react to their rejection in different ways, there is a tendency to show emotional instability, restlessness, attention-getting behavior, overactivity, rebellion and delinquency. Often the children are lonely, fearful, unhappy and insecure.[22] This insecurity carries over to later life, and the rejected individual has difficulty accepting and expressing love. Several studies have shown that those who were rejected as children in turn reject their own youngsters.[23]

3. Parental overprotection. The individual who is "tied to his mother's apron strings" is an object of ridicule in our society. Sometimes a parent, usually a mother, hovers over a child, protects him from every potential danger, smothers

him with affection, makes decisions for him, and treats him as "my baby" even when he has grown to adulthood. A protected individual such as this has little opportunity to "stand on his own two feet," fend for himself, or develop his potentialities and autonomy. Instead, he complies to powerful parental demands and becomes submissive. In school he is a "sissy," and throughout life he is likely to be passive, nervous, socially inadequate, insecure, and unable to handle even mild amounts of stress. Perhaps we could say that the overprotected child is like a tree which has grown up in a warm, glass-enclosed greenhouse. When the tree is moved outside, it is adversely influenced by winds and weather changes which leave other trees unharmed.

4. Parental overindulgence and permissiveness. This occurs when one or both parents give the child whatever he wants, regardless of how unreasonable or infantile the request. When a child is "spoiled" like this, he grows up to expect that adults other than his parents will continue to comply with his wishes. These overindulged people are selfish, demanding, irresponsible and stubborn. It is difficult for them to form warm relationships with other people because human relationships must be on their own terms. As adults, they are irritated by authority and become angry with anyone who refuses to abide by their wishes. Sometimes they will "pout" or throw a temper tantrum and, as one might expect, their ability to withstand stress is usually low.

5. Rigid, perfectionistic demands. Under the guise of "good discipline," parents sometimes dominate their children, impose strict and rigid rules, and make demands that children are unable to meet. The child with limited ability who is expected to get high grades, for example, or the active youngster who must always be a model of good behavior in church, eventually concludes that he "can't do it, so why try?" Such children often become insecure, anxious, and plagued by guilt feelings. Frequently they are hostile

37

and rebellious, but many times they develop rigid, restricted personalities which show an overconformity to rules or regulations and an inability to tolerate nonconformity in others. Once again, the ability to withstand precipitating stress is low.

Regretfully, such behavior is often typical of the children of Christians. Scripture instructs parents to train their children (Pr. 22:6) and this includes discipline (Pr. 23:13). But to make cold, rigid, perfectionistic demands which are beyond the child's capacity to obey, is to train up a child who will be a legalistic, neurotic, and perhaps a resentful Christian. Paul recognized that such discipline would adversely influence children. "Don't keep on scolding and nagging your children, making them angry and resentful," he wrote. "Rather, bring them up with the loving discipline the Lord himself approves, with suggestions and godly advice" (Eph. 6:4, *Living Bible*).

If a child is to develop into a mentally healthy adult, he must have a clear view of the behavior that is expected of him. Infractions should be consistently, rapidly, and firmly dealt with, but the child should know that the parents still love him in spite of his behavior. As he grows older and more mature, freedom and discussion of rules can be allowed.

*Early family disharmony.* The atmosphere at home significantly influences how a child will react to stress later in life. When the family atmosphere is characterized by constant bickering, (as it was in Mike's home), frequent quarreling, sarcasm, criticism, and degrading jokes about family members, children often become insecure and anxious. As the child gets older he seeks to get away from the unpleasant home situation; and when he encounters stress in the world, he reacts as he had been taught at home—with an aggression that sometimes becomes delinquency.

*Early trauma.* The sudden death of a loved one, the witnessing of a bad accident, the experience of sudden and unexpected danger—these are examples of traumatic situations which often lead to a psychological shock reaction. Such experiences are likely to leave all of us temporarily tense and insecure, but for some persons the shock is so great that there follows a more permanent insecurity with a lowered ability to withstand stress. The individual who survives a serious airplane crash, for example, may be nervous and highly sensitive to stress for many years.

*Inadequate learning.* To a very large extent, behavior is the result of learning. The clothes we wear, the language we speak, the way in which we worship, the eating utensils we use, the specific foods we like, and the way we interact in a social situation, are all the result of past learning. Since so much basic learning takes place early in life, these first few years are of crucial importance in the development of later emotional stability.

Sometimes, however, early learning fails to equip the individual to meet the stresses and pressures of later life. Many people are highly inadequate in social situations because they "don't know what to say" or have never learned how to interact comfortably with others. High school students often experience considerable uncertainty, insecurity, and social rejection if they have never learned how to act on a date. When the academic pressures become intense, college students sometimes panic and become anxious because they have never learned how to study or how to organize their time. In each of these examples, the individual is ill-prepared to face the stresses of life because of inadequate training. As we shall see in later chapters, much psychological counseling involves teaching people how to meet the challenges of life and how to overcome the insecuity that results from inadequate learning.

*Individual differences in perception.* The way in which we see a situation also determines how we will react. The little child who is afraid in a dark house at night might be very startled to hear a windowpane rattle. The rattling may simply be due to the wind, but the child, in his fears, *perceived* the situation as being much more dangerous. Likewise, the soldier who enters enemy territory maintains a heightened vigilance because he views the situation as dangerous, even though the enemy may be nowhere in sight.

This is one of the reasons why people react differently to similar stress situations. To address a congregation of one thousand people may be perceived as an exciting challenge by one preacher, but another pastor may quiver with stage fright. Probably these differences in perception can be traced to differences in our past learning. The fact remains, however, that an individual's ability to tolerate a stress depends on the way in which he views both the stress situation and his own ability to meet the demands of the situation.

SOCIOLOGICAL PREDISPOSING FACTORS

Within recent years, research by sociologists, anthropologists and social psychologists has demonstrated that the the cultural setting in which one lives has a profound influence on the amount of stress that one can tolerate. Important sociological influences include one's occupation, social class, cultural group, and place of residence. In addition, one's sex, marital status, race, and religious beliefs can be significantly related to stress tolerance, depending on the cultural or geographical area in which one lives.

*Occupation.* A man's job occupies a large portion of his time and has a significant bearing on his standard of living, socioeconomic status, choice of friends, prestige, and leisure activities. According to Thorpe and his associates, unless an individual "is reasonably well-satisfied with his work, he cannot possibly achieve a healthy personal adjustment."[24]

Unfortunately, many people are not satisfied with their work. Some feel that they have made the wrong vocational choice. Many are involved in working conditions characterized by monotony, low morale, employee friction, long hours, periodic layoffs, poor wages, low prestige, and/or little opportunity for advancement. For such people, a change might appear desirable, but this is often impossible because of lack of training or opportunity. As a result, the individual is inextricably tied to a miserable job. Of course he is dissatisfied, and this dissatisfaction is likely to be accompanied by increased tension, irritability, insecurity, and a low opinion of himself. It should not come as a surprise to learn that such persons have a low ability to meet stress.

*Social class.* A number of sociological studies have demonstrated conclusively that psychological abnormality is closely related to socioeconomic class. In the 1950s for example, two Yale professors conducted a comprehensive study of a community in New Haven, Connecticut.[25] They attempted to arrive at an individual's socioeconomic class by considering three factors: area of residence, occupation and education. Five major social-class groupings were identified, with Class I being the highest class, and Class V the lowest. Following this, the researchers determined the number of people in each class who were undergoing treatment by a psychiatrist or being cared for in a psychiatric institution. Table 1-2 summarizes the findings.

*Table 1-2*

**Relation of social class to normal and psychiatric populations***

| Class | Percent of Normal Population | Percent of Psychiatric Population |
|---|---|---|
| I (Highest) | 3.0 ⎤ | 1.0 ⎤ |
| II | 8.4 ⎦ 11.4 | 7.0 ⎦ 8.0 |
| III | 20.4 | 13.7 |
| IV | 49.8 ⎤ | 40.1 ⎤ |
| V(Lowest) | 18.4 ⎦ 68.2 | 38.2 ⎦ 78.3 |
| | 100.0 | 100.0 |
| Number of persons studied | 236,940 | 1891 |

*Adapted from A. B. Hollingshead and F. C. Redlich, *Social Class and Mental Illness: A Community Study*, p. 199.

It will be noted that whereas 11.4 percent of the population was from classes I and II only 8 percent of the psychiatric patients came from these classes. At the other end of the scale, 62.8 percent of the population were in classes IV and V, but 78.3 percent of the psychiatric cases came from these classes. Similar research conducted in other parts of the country has supported these findings.

Apparently membership in a social class to some extent determines a person's ability to cope with stress. Several reasons could account for this. First, there is evidence that child-rearing practices differ among social classes.[26] Middle-class mothers are especially demanding of their children, and such pressures could influence subsequent stress tolerance. Second, there may be class differences in self-perception. Perhaps lower-class people have a greater tendency to see themselves as being inadequate and unable to cope with stress. Third, since past learning is so important there may be class differences in the adequacy of one's preparation for coping with stress. Finally, our culture is still highly oriented toward "getting ahead." Lower-class people may show a greater susceptibility to stress because of competition, insecurity, and strong frustration when they are not able to rise in society. The lower classes also contain those persons whose mobility has been downward. People who have slipped on the social scale tend to have a high rate of mental illness.[27]

Of course membership in the lower social class does not condemn one to psychological abnormality. There are both emotionally disturbed and emotionally healthy people in all classes, but the added frustrations and difficulties of lower-class living reduce one's ability to deal with stress.

*Cultural group.* The Hutterites are a small religious sect living in a number of scattered communities throughout the North American Midwest. Numbering about 9,000 these people marry only within their sect, raise large families, and support themselves with a highly mechanized form of agriculture. Their way of life is simple and group-centered. Jewelry, art, radio, television and movies are all considered sinful. The women have similar hair styles, everyone wears the same kind of clothes, and homes are furnished alike. Bills are paid from a community treasury, property is owned by the group, and even cooking is done in large quantities to provide similar meals for everybody. There is much emphasis on religion, duty to God, strict morality, and the importance of showing little aggression. As one might expect, the Hutterites are strict pacifists.

When this group was studied a few years ago, it was found that no one had ever been in a mental hospital. Suicide, divorce or persistent marital strife were rare, while murder, arson, physical assault and sex crimes were completely nonexistent. Indeed, it appeared that the stable and protective culture had made the people immune to mental disorders.

Closer study revealed, however, that the Hutterites were not free from psychological disorders; they just showed a unique type of abnormality. For some members, the group's unwillingness to tolerate aggression and individuality apparently had led to self-blame, guilt feelings, and a tendency to withdraw into a state of depression. When a Hutterite did display abnormality, the group rallied to his support and provided a protective environment which made hospitalization unnecessary.[28]

Numerous studies of different societies have supported the finding that both the prevalence and the type of abnormality differ from culture to culture. A number of reasons could be suggested to explain this. Cultural differences in religious beliefs, social expectations, and practices, for example, could have a bearing on how an individual handles stress. Also important might be the extent to which there is group support for the individual, the prevalence of competition within the society, and the freedom with which different cultures permit an individual to express sexual, aggressive or other impulses.

43

*Place of residence.* People who live in the country are less likely to enter mental hospitals than are city people. While this may be due to the greater number of treatment facilities in the city (so that city people find it easier to go for treatment), it is also possible that there is less stress in rural areas. Certainly people who live in the country face a different kind of stress than that encountered by city dwellers.

Even within the city there are differences in the prevalence of psychological disorders. People in slum areas show greater abnormality than those who live in neighborhoods with low-cost private homes. These neighborhoods in turn report more psychological abnormality than suburban residential areas. Of course, the part of the city in which one lives is largely determined by one's social class. For this reason it is unlikely that the neighborhood by itself is a very important predisposing factor.

*Minority group membership.* People who are members of racial or ethnic minority groups generally show greater evidence of abnormality than those who are not in minority groups. In the United States, for example, mental hospital admission rates are higher for blacks than for whites. Foreign-born people show a greater tendency to be hospitalized than do the native-born. Probably these different hospital rates are due to the fact that members of the minority groups often live in states of perpetual tension, fear, frustration and insecurity. This has a wearing effect after a while and reduces one's ability to withstand stress. [29]

Horace Cayton revealed some of this tension when he described a Southern trip which he made several years ago with a white man and his wife:

> We rode on that trip as conspirators in an enemy country. Each meal presented itself as a challenge, a battle to be fought, and each success was greeted by us as a victory over the enemy. As lunch time drew near we were all silent with a tension which descended over the entire car. Would we,

44

under some pretext, be able to eat together? If not, could I find a Negro restaurant? If there were no Negro restaurants, should I go to the kitchen of the white hotel and pretend to be their chauffeur or should I remain in the car and have them bring sandwiches to me? At night came the question of finding a place to sleep. . . .

Even normal body functions presented a problem. They could be performed. . .only with considerable opposition delay, annoyance, and irritation. Could I drink from the water fountain at the filling station? Would there be provisions for washing my hands or face? If a toilet was not marked "white only" or "colored" dare I use it?

Every mile of the road we encountered difficulties, hindrances, and frictions which bothered, annoyed, and infuriated. All of these impeded our progress and upon all we expended energy which detracted from our pleasure and exhausted us physically and emotionally. Added to this friction was of course the fear which arose out of both the real danger in the environment. As a Negro, in performing the simple act of living, I found myself irritated, by the frictions set up against me, endangered by real possibilities of harm, and the target of all of those barbs, indignities, heartaches, and the thousand shocks that black flesh is heir to.[30]

For the black man the frustrations still persist, even though conditions in the United States have changed considerably during the past decade.

*Sex.* Are psychological breakdowns more common among women or among men? A national mental-health survey conducted in the late 1950s found that women are more likely to report that they are experiencing psychological distress and are more likely to seek help with their problems.[31] However, this greater willingness on the part of women to *express* their problems does not necessarily mean that the women *experience* more problems than men. Apparently there is little difference between the sexes as far as frequency of mental disorders is concerned, although there is some difference as to the type of problem. Men worry about their jobs and economic problems, whereas women are more concerned with children and family matters.

45

*Marital status.* Married people have the highest mental-health rating, widows and widowers . come next, single persons are third, and divorced persons show the poorest adjustment. Several reasons have been given to account for these differences. It may be that the married person has people to care for him and is less likely to be hospitalized than the single or divorced person. Perhaps there are stabilizing factors in married life that prevent psychological breakdown. More likely, the unmarried and divorced people who enter mental hospitals have developed some characteristics that, prior to hospitalization, had made them both a poor marriage risk and persons with low ability to tolerate stress.

*Religious affiliation.* Surveys have shown that people who attend church regularly report less psychological stress than those who attend less frequently.[32] Perhaps the church provides religious and/or group support which enables attenders to handle a greater amount of stress.

Other studies have compared the mental health of Protestants, Catholics and Jews, but such surveys are not very meaningful because of the vast differences within these groups. A "Protestant," for example, could refer to one who is evangelical or liberal, Unitarian or Pentecostal, active or an occasional church-attender. Comparable differences exist within the Catholic and Jewish categories. A finer breakdown of these three groups would give a better indication of the extent to which religious affiliation influences ability to withstand stress, but such a study has not yet been reported.

### SPIRITUAL PREDISPOSING FACTORS

*Lack of meaning to life.* Following World War II a book was published describing the experiences of a psychiatrist from Vienna who had spent three years at Auschwitz and other Nazi prison camps. The psychiatrist, Dr. Viktor E. Frankl, has subsequently been hailed both as a "successor to Freud" and as "the greatest living psychiatrist." From the time he entered the prison camp and was literally stripped naked, until he was liberated (and learned that his parents, brother, and wife had all died), Dr. Frankl observed his own reactions and those of his fellow prisoners. He discovered that many of the prisoners saw no meaning to life, had no reason to live, and no faith in the future. These were the people who "fell victim to the camp's degenerating influences" and gave up the struggle to keep alive. In contrast, the people who had some meaning in life, who were willing to help others, who could appreciate the beauties of nature (even if only in the form of the sunset viewed through a crack in the wall), who could see some purpose for the suffering— these were the people who maintained psychological stability in spite of their intense suffering.

As a result of his experiences, Frankl came to the conclusion that every man is searching for meaning. "There is nothing in the world," he wrote, ". . .that would so effectively help one to survive even the worst situations, as the knowledge that there is meaning in one's life. There is much wisdom in the words of Nietzsche: 'he who has a *why* to live for, can bear most any *how*.'"* Undoubtedly it is true that the individual whose life is meaningless and without purpose has a lower ability to tolerate stress and a greater predisposition to psychological abnormality.

*Lack of belief in Christ.* Although he is not a Christian, Frankl recognizes that when an individual embraces some

---

*Frankl believes that the desire to rewrite a book gave him a purpose for living during his years in prison. When he entered Auschwitz, a completed manuscript was taken from him, and he was determined to get out of prison and rewrite this book. "Certainly, my deep concern to write this manuscript anew helped me to survive the rigors of camp. For instance, when I fell ill with typhus fever I jotted down on little scraps of paper many notes intended to enable me to rewrite the manuscript, should I live to the day of liberation. I am sure that this reconstruction of my lost manuscript in the dark barracks of a Bavarian concentration camp assisted me in overcoming the danger of collapse." (V.E. Frankl, *Man's Search for Meaning*, p. 164).

kind of faith there is a resulting increase in his ability to withstand stress. According to one of Frankl's followers, "The truly religious person whose spiritual needs are fully satisfied by his beliefs should not be in need of therapy." [33]

Perhaps most readers would agree that a person who has faith in a religious, political, economic or other system is probably able to cope more effectively with stress than is the individual who does not have faith in anything. As Christians, however, we believe that faith in the Christ of the Scriptures is superior to all other belief systems. When Christ and the Holy Spirit enter the life of a believer and take control, the individual develops qualities of love, joy, peace, patience, kindness, goodness, faithfulness, gentleness and self-control (Gal. 5:22-23). There is a change in values, assurance of an eternal life spent with Christ, and potential for an "abundant life" here on earth. This gives our very existence a meaning which is not shaken by death or suffering. As a Christian, for example, the apostle Paul found life and death to be equally attractive (Phil. 1:20-24). Of course, other religions make claims similar to those in the Bible and, in so doing, the followers of these systems feel a greater purpose for life. But it is only in the life of a Christian that we encounter a supernatural force which gives power to meet the stresses and seeming inconsistencies of life. The existence of this God of the Bible cannot be proven scientifically or logically, but His existence is revealed in Scripture and must be experienced to be known.

At this point it must be emphasized that *whereas nonbelief in Christ can lower one's ability to cope with stress, and whereas belief in Christ can increase one's ability to withstand pressure, it does not follow that the Christian is immune from developing a psychological abnormality.* The Bible makes no promise of psychological health as a result of conversion. It does not guarantee that the believer will experience ecstatic joy or perpetual freedom from turmoil. Indeed, the abundant life includes unpleasant stressful experiences. To become a Christian changes one's ability to withstand stress, but it is no guarantee of perpetual psychological stability.

*Fear.* Bertrand Russell, who was a caustic but influential critic of Christianity, once stated that fear is the basis of all religion—fear of the mysterious, fear of defeat, fear of death. [34] Most of us would consider such a statement to be an exaggeration, but we must admit that many people become Christians out of a fear of death, hell, and even God. The writer recalls hearing an evangelistic sermon in which the speaker told his audience, "If I could scare you into becoming a Christian, I'd do it." While such devotion to the cause of Christ might be admired, it should also be recognized that scaring an individual has no scriptural precedent and can be a precipitator of psychological breakdown.

Sometimes preachers, even those who have been used by God to bring many to a knowledge of Christ, get carried away with their imaginations. Jonathan Edward's sermon *Sinners in the Hand of an Angry God* is an example:

> The God that holds you over the pit of hell much as we hold a spider, or loathsome insect over a fire, abhors you, and is dreadfully provoked. His wrath towards you burns like fire.

People who respond to such preaching often have no concept of the love of God and live a Christian life which is characterized by rigidity, insecurity and perpetual fear. Their beliefs are likely to be rigid and legalistic, they exhibit a superior manner toward those who do not fit their "standards," and their prayers become a pious "process of dickering for favors on the basis of credits gained through devotional activity, church attendance, tithing, and participation in programs of Christian service."[35] In themselves, these activities are highly desirable, but many Christians who have an immature faith perform these acts

49

to rid themselves of anxieties. Regretfully, there appear to be many believers who have this kind of faith, and for them there is no real joy of Christian living. Instead of possessing a faith which brings a greater resistance to stress, such persons are like dynamite, ready to explode with the slightest provocation.

## CHANGES IN THE ORGANISM

Acting singly or in combination, the many influences which have been discussed in this chapter bring about changes in the individual. As shown in the center box of Figure 1-1, the changes are primarily of two types. First, the individual's perception changes. As a result of his experiences he comes to see or think of the world and of himself in a different way. If he is seriously hurt in an accident, for example, he recognizes that his body has been injured and he is physically helpless and in pain. If he is embarrassed in a social situation, he perceives that he has created a social blunder. If he is converted to Christianity, he recognizes that his life is in some way different. These changes in the way of looking at himself and his world may occur slowly or suddenly. Since an individual often acts according to the facts *as he sees them*, these changes in perception bring automatic changes in behavior.[36] An outsider may think that the actions of another person are pretty foolish or inappropriate, but the outsider sees things differently than the *behaver*. When the predisposing and precipitating factors change, an individual's view of the world and of himself changes, and behavior alterations invariably follow.

The second kind of change is in the physiological, sociological, psychological and spiritual functioning of the individual. If one receives a blow on the head, his body must react with pain, brain damage, or perhaps a loss of consciousness. If a tornado strikes, perhaps fear and prayer will result. These changes in behavior form the symptoms or indicators of abnormality which are considered in the next chapter.

## SUMMARY

The causes of abnormal behavior are extremely complex. In order to fully understand the reasons for breakdown, one must consider both the stresses which an individual encounters (precipitating factors) and the state of the person at the time of stress (predisposing factors).

The precipitating factors which cause the person to "break down" can come from a number of sources. There can be biological stresses, such as the experience of serious disease or the taking of a drug; psychological frustrations, conflicts or pressures; social stresses such as war, accidents, or marriage problems; and spiritual pressures related to a strong sense of guilt or sin. Singly or together, these and other stresses can be so overwhelming to the individual that he is unable to act normally.

It two people experience the same amount of stress, however, it does not follow that they will both collapse under the strain. There are large individual differences in the amount of pressure that we can withstand. These differences can be attributed to biological factors, including one's heredity or health; psychological factors, such as early childhood experiences; sociological factors like social class or marital status; and spiritual factors, such as one's goals in life or commitment to Christ.

Alone or in combination, these factors can influence the individual's behavior in at least two ways. His perception or way of looking at the world and at himself can change (this will bring about a change in his behavior), or there will be a change in his biological, psychological, sociological and/or spiritual functioning. If these changes can be seen, we can often get a clue to the causes of behavior. The signs and symptoms which we look for are discussed in the following chapters.

# 2

# Signs, Symptoms, and Classification of Abnormal Behavior

Kenneth J., an eighteen-year-old single boy, was transferred from jail, where he had been held for disturbing the peace, to the psychiatric wing of the hospital of a small midwestern town where he had lived with his parents. . . .

One evening, five months before his hospital admission, Kenneth attended a movie with a new acquaintance. Afterward he went to the acquaintance's room in a boardinghouse, where both began drinking wine and eventually engaged in a homosexual act. Kenneth went to confession early the next morning, but felt that his sins were not forgiven. He began to worry about this, became depressed, even more withdrawn than previously, lost his appetite, and became diarrheic. He also began to speak of an invasion of the earth by men from other planets, and left his own room to take up residence in the tool shed in back of his house. He was taken to the family physician, and appeared well-mannered until his mother joined him, when he became irritable and quarreled with her. Medication was prescribed but he didn't take it, because he felt it was poison, and did not keep his return appointment. Kenneth became preoccupied with religious questions and expressed the fear of burning in hell. He spent many hours in the tool shed burning odd objects, such as paper, underclothes, books, and the like. Once, when burning a small reproduction of a painting of Christ in his furnace, he heard a voice cry, "Whosoever shall burn me will be thrice saved." He refused to eat apples because he felt it was sinful to do so. After a period in which he continually awoke in the middle of the night screaming that a huge dragon was after him, he took to staying awake all night and sleeping in the day. He also began to draw crosses on walls,

53

mirrors, doors, and wherever he found a flat surface.

One month before his admission Kenneth stopped drawing crosses, but started to say that he hated his family, who were sinners, dirt, and not his real family at all. Believing that he belonged to a celestial family, he attacked the people posing as his mother and father, and stopped eating at home lest his mother should poison him. He attended church five times every Sunday, and pored over religious books during the week. When passing women on the street he knew were sinners, he detected a foul and sickening odor. Then he declared that he was Jesus, was born 2,000 years ago and had a wound on the palm of each hand. . . .He began to wander in his back yard at night, praying aloud and shouting that the world was coming to an end. The neighbors reported this to the police, who came to investigate, and when he informed them that he was Jesus, they took him to jail. He resented this and said, "Some day all the jails in the world will crumble." The next morning he was transferred to the psychiatric wing of the local hospital.

When he was interviewed upon admission Kenneth expressed the feeling that the whole world had become a dream. His affect was generally flat, and he complained of numerous vague somatic ailments, such as being stuck by a needle. He was withdrawn with other patients and obsequious with the personnel. . . .His answers to questions were often incoherent after the first sentence when he would ruminate about being born 2,000 years ago. He felt that God was within him, and especially when looking in a mirror, he could feel his hair and beard growing. He also believed that he had a rib missing. Kenneth further believed that he would soon control everything, including electricity, and that people would run from him. While listening to music he heard angels calling him Jesus. Shadows on the ward were misinterpreted as snakes trying to kill him. This preoccupation with his delusions and hallucinations made Kenneth more seclusive on the ward, and he would only interact with others when they approached him. At the supper table he would eat with his fingers and chant, and laugh inappropriately at remarks made by himself and others. [1]


If any of us had seen Kenneth during or immediately prior to his hospitalization, we probably would have realized that the boy was seriously disturbed. Belief that one is Christ, fear that the world is crawling with deadly snakes, the hearing of angelic voices, and the opinion that one will control the whole world—all such behavior is clearly abnormal.

Because of their unusual behavior, many disturbed people, like Kenneth, are easily recognized. There are numerous others, however, whose problems may be severe but whose symptoms are not nearly so apparent. Visitors to mental hospitals often discover this when they meet patients who seem to be quite normal but who are disturbed enough to have been institutionalized. Even trained counselors have difficulty in detecting abnormality at times because people are so skilled in hiding their problems.

Psychological abnormality is like a cancer; the sooner it is detected, the sooner it can be treated and its growth arrested. Rarely, however, do psychologists, psychiatrists or other professionals see the abnormality when it is beginning. By the time an individual comes or is brought in for help, the behavior disorder is usually well-developed. In contrast, when he knows what to look for, the church leader is in a unique position for spotting problems in their early stages. He has frequent and regular contact with his people, is freer to discuss problems with them, and is able to visit in their homes. No psychologist has any of these privileges. If the early signs of trouble can be detected by someone in the church, then the problems can be dealt with sooner and more effectively. Perhaps a pastor or Sunday school teacher could have recognized Kenneth J.'s problems before they became so severe.

## SIGNS AND SYMPTOMS OF ABNORMAL BEHAVIOR

Included in Figure 1-1 is a list of the signs of abnormality.* Some of these are present at all times in all of our lives, but

*This figure appears in chap. 1. Table 2-1 (page 71) is a good approximation of the relevant part of Fig. 1-1.

*the signs become danger signals when several are apparent at the same time, when their presence indicates a change from previous behavior, and when they persist over a period of time.* Like the causes of behavior disorders, the symptoms can also be of a physical, psychological, social or spiritual nature.

PHYSICAL SYMPTOMS

To a large extent, physical and psychological functioning are intertwined. When a person is physically sick or in great pain, for example, the illness often influences his actions and thinking. If we miss a meal or don't get enough sleep, most of us discover that we are irritable or hard to get along with. Indeed, it is difficult to think of any physical condition that does not bring at least some change in behavior.

On the other hand, psychological states such as insecurity, grief, anger, anxiety or excitement can bring significant changes in the body's physical functioning. We acknowledge this when we use such familiar expressions as "worried sick" or "scared to death." It is well-known that pressured businessmen sometimes develop ulcers and that frightened grooms occasionally pass out in front of the preacher. According to several estimates, over half of all patients who consult physicians have symptoms and illnesses which result from and are expressions of emotional disturbances.

The physical problems that arise as a result of psychological tension are usually called *psychophysiological* or *psychosomatic* reactions. These may include ulcers, nightmares, vomiting, continual indigestion, constipation, diarrhea, frequent urination, skin rashes, headaches, asthma, hay fever, profuse sweating, backaches, inability to sleep (insomnia), inability to stay awake, and sleepwalking. Of course, these symptoms are not always psychosomatic; often they have some real physical cause. Only a qualified physician can accurately determine whether symptoms are physically or psychologically produced, but the church leader can be alert to the presence of such symptoms and can encourage his counselees (the people who are being counseled) to have routine medical checkups. This is especially true if the counselee complains of pain or sickness.

The relationship between physical symptoms and psychological disturbances is discussed more fully in chapter 4.

PSYCHOLOGICAL INDICATIONS

A number of commonly used techniques enable all of us to deal with the stresses and frustrations of everyday life. We can, for example, attack the source of our frustrations, withdraw from a situation, seek a compromise solution, or rely on one or more defensive mechanisms. If used occasionally, these types of behavior are common and quite normal.

Sometimes, however, an individual will rely on these techniques to such an extent that he cannot adapt to new or different situations. There is an overdependence on the behavior which normal people would use in moderation when handling stress. Sometimes, for example, the person under stress withdraws, not into casual daydreaming, but into a fantasy world which has no contact with outside reality. Instead of using an occasional excuse for his actions (we all do this), the person under stress may make a habit of telling highly improbable stories and claiming that these are the truth. Instead of praying and seeking God's help to overcome some crisis, the person may develop all kinds of strange ideas about the influence of demons or angels in his life. [2] Abnormal behavior, therefore, is not something new and different; it consists primarily of normal behavior taken to extremes.

The following are psychological signs that may indicate abnormality:

*Faulty perception.* The sense organs in the body, such as the eyes, ears or nose, normally receive stimulations from the environment. These stimulations are in turn relayed through the nervous system to the brain. By this process

57

we are able to perceive objects in space, recognize faces, hear noises, or experience hot, cold, pain, smells, textures and tastes. When problems are present, however, these perceptual abilities are sometimes altered. Such alternations can occur in at least four ways:

1. Reduced sensitivity. Psychologically produced blindness, hearing losses for which there is no known organic cause, or reduction in the ability to feel pain are examples of reduced sensitivity. This is one way in which an individual withdraws from the world and its stresses.

Peter was a 37-year-old married man who was brought to the clinic by an older brother. The youngest in a family of five boys, Peter was the only one who had not succeeded in life. His eldest brother was a bank president. Another pastored a large and growing Presbyterian church, and the remaining two brothers were very successful businessmen.

Peter had had a number of jobs and most recently had been in a business partnership. When the business was in danger of failing, however, the partner ran away with the profits and Peter lost everything. After another period of unemployment he finally got a job as a truck driver, but when he went on his first assignment he drove off the road several times because "my eyes kept going shut."

When Peter came to my office he reported that his eyes no longer remained open by themselves. As he talked, he held each eyelid open with his fingers. Whenever he removed his fingers, the eyes went shut. Peter's concerned brothers had arranged for a complete physical, neurological and opthamological examination, but all of the doctors gave the same report—there was nothing physically wrong. Apparently the eye problem was psychologically caused. By having his "seeing problem" Peter got sympathy and attention from his busy and successful older brothers, and because his sight difficulties persisted, he did not have to face the prospect of going to work where he would risk failure and humiliation again.

After intensive psychological treatment, Peter gained a new self-confidence and self-esteem. When this happened, the eye problem slowly disappeared.

58

2. Increased sensitivity. Sometimes a person may complain that a light is too bright or a room is too noisy, even though others agree that the stimulation in the environment is not excessive. Here the person is usually tense or on edge and unable to tolerate even minor stimulations.

3. Distorted sensitivity. This refers to a misinterpretation of stimuli and is normally called an *illusion*. The child who cycles home on a dark winter evening may hear a rustle of leaves and momentarily jump to the conclusion that this indicates danger. Illusions such as this are common and quite normal, but when a person concludes that television announcers are watching him from the TV screen or that newspapers are conveying private messages to him, this is clearly abnormal. In the case history at the beginning of the chapter, Kenneth J. demonstrated an illusion when he misinterpreted the shadows on the ward and thought they were snakes trying to kill him.

4. Hallucinations. This term refers to a perception which takes place when there is no external stimulation. Except when we are dreaming or under the influence of drugs, normal people rarely hear voices or see individuals and objects that are not present. Disturbed people sometimes experience such perceptions, however, and respond to the people that they see or the voices they hear. Kenneth J. for example, heard voices and experienced a "foul and sickening odor" when he passed women who he "knew were sinners" on the street.

Sometimes the nature of a specific misperception gives the counselor a clue to the reason for the abnormality. One lady lost her sense of smell, for example, when her son began to drink heavily. When she couldn't smell alcohol, she was spared the pain of facing the reality of her son's drinking. By asking himself, "Why would it be important to lose one's smell?" the counselor was able to get some clues about the issue which was bothering the woman. A church leader should know about these perceptual signs, even though it is only on rare occasions—if at all—that he would be likely to encounter them.

*Distorted thinking.* Thinking can be distorted in its content and/or progression. In considering the *content* of an individual's thinking, we want to know if his thoughts "make sense." Many disturbed people are of the opinion that their thinking is quite logical, but others disagree. Kenneth J.'s conclusion that he would soon "control everything, including electricity" and his idea that he was born 2,000 years ago, may have made sense to him, but they are foolish to anyone else and give clear evidence of distorted thinking.

The content of distorted thinking can include obsessions, phobias or delusions. Obsessions refer to the persistent recurrence of some unpleasant impulse or thought. The individual who can't get rid of the idea that someone is "out to get me" or that "I'm going to kill somebody" is experiencing an obsession. Phobias are irrational fears that are maintained even in the absence of real danger. Claustrophobia, or fear of enclosed places, is well-known. Other phobias include fear of open spaces, blood, snakes, heights, darkness, storms or crowds. Of course, so many well-adjusted people experience mild phobias that this hardly seems to be a clue to abnormality. It is usually when they are intense or combined with other signs that phobias indicate the possible existence of a problem. Delusions refer to false beliefs that are not consistent with an individual's knowledge and experience. Delusions of persecution occur when an individual believes, without justification, that other people are intent upon harming him in some way. Delusions of grandeur refer to an exaggerated belief in one's own importance. Kenneth J.'s belief that he was Jesus is an example.

In addition to these distortions in the content of thinking, there can also be distortions in the *progression* or sequence of thought. The following is an excerpt from an interview with a hospital patient who was asked about her illness:

No, I never was crazy, a little nervous. Look at my teeth.
I came here to have my teeth fixed. We're going to have a
strawberry party now. Yesterday I heard voices. They said,
"I ran to the drugstore and I am going home tomorrow."
I heard J. B. Schott's voice and it came from up here in the
air. We've got 39 banks on Market Street. We've got lots of
property. Say, take me home and I'll give you three laundry
bags. I'm 29 and a half. Now I want you to get me ten apples—
ten of your most beautiful apples and two dozen lemons.
Now listen, if I get you some pineapple will you preserve it? [3]

In this example, the patient drifts from topic to topic,
and shows no logical sequence of thought. Her discussion
of fruit is far removed from the original topic. Less extreme
forms of this behavior include prolonged talking about one
topic, and a tendency to meander or be easily distracted.

Like each of the signs listed in this chapter, distorted
thinking is not always present or apparent. Sometimes a
very disturbed individual can converse easily and with ideas
that appear quite rational. Such people are so sure of their
faulty perceptions and distorted conclusions that they can
argue very convincingly. Sometimes sympathetic counselors
are "taken in" by plausible stories which later turn out to
be highly imaginary distortions of the truth.

*Faulty emotional expression.* If we did not experience
emotions, our lives would probably be drab, colorless, and
little more than machines which operate from day to day in
a mechanical fashion. But we are not like this. Instead, we
are all creatures of emotion. We experience and have learned
how to express joy and sorrow, pleasure and pain, happiness and sadness, elation and discouragement, excitement
and apathy, love and hate, pride and shame, delight and
horror. However, the disturbed person's feelings and expressions of emotion often differ considerably from those of
more normal people. Indeed, so common are these disturbances in emotional expression that abnormal behavior
is often referred to as an "emotional disorder."

At times emotional reactions are also termed "affective experiences" or, more simply, "affects." The church leader should be aware of the following affective signs, two or three of which will appear in the same individual, while other people may show one sign only—or none:

1. Flat affect. Some people give the impression that they experience no emotion at all. They do not laugh at jokes, apparently are unmoved by sad situations, and show no evidence of anxiety, excitement, discouragement, or any other common feelings. Such individuals convey a "blah— couldn't-care-less" attitude. In the case history, Kenneth J. was described as being a patient whose "affect was generally flat."

2. Elation or euphoria. These terms refer to an exaggerated feeling of well-being which takes control of the individual and gives him the confident assurance that everything in life is wonderful. A popular song of a few years ago expressed this feeling: "Things look great, things look swell. . .everything's coming up roses." One feels "on top of the world" all the time.

This euphoria is different from the joy that is experienced by Christians. As described in Scripture, joy apparently is a deep feeling of security and well-being which comes to the life that is controlled by the Holy Spirit (Gal. 5:22). Such inner joy is based on our belief in an omnipotent God and it differs from euphoria in at least two ways. First, joy does not blind us to the realities of life. Paul experienced this abiding joy even though he recognized that life was difficult and that there were people who hated him and his message. Second, Christian joy is deep-seated, but euphoria is not. The disturbed person's elation is very shallow and if he is frustrated in some way, he may quickly (although temporarily) become irritable and unhappy.

3. Depression. At times, all of us become discouraged or "blue" because of frustrations and difficulties in our lives. Such discouragement is very common and usually of short

duration. However, when an individual experiences feelings of despair and despondency which are of long duration and without logical explanation, this is a sign of maladjustment. The person usually reports that he is worried about something (such as health, job, family or future), and he describes himself as being sad, unhappy, worthless, and/or sinful. Sometimes the depression is accompanied by frequent crying, while often there is also a feeling of hopelessness and self-deprecation which leads one to consider suicide.

4. Emotional variability. Each of us experiences emotional "ups and downs" as we encounter the joys and frustrations of everyday living. Such reactions become indicators of possible abnormality when, compared with other people in similar situations, an individual experiences ups and downs which are of greater intensity and which last for longer periods of time.

Sometimes these extremes of emotional behavior occur without any apparent cause. One author has suggested that emotional variability can be seen in the person who "blows his top for no good reason at all," weeps when there appears to be no reason for weeping, or is easily "triggered off" into a strong emotional outburst or temper tantrum. (Ramsey, 1963). It is a good idea to note the situation which gives rise to these emotional displays. Often such a situation may give a clue to the cause of the disturbance.

5. Inappropriate affect. This refers to emotional behavior which is different from that experienced by most people. The person who giggles at a funeral or responds with tears upon hearing of some humorous incident is showing affect which is not appropriate.

6. Fear and anxiety. It is normal for a person to experience a feeling of discomfort and threat in the face of new and difficult situations. Indeed, anxiety could be thought of as something good which mobilizes us for action and enables us to prepare for some anticipated stress. How many of us would have passed our examinations in school

if we had not be motivated by the anxiety that examinations bring?

Nevertheless, at times anxiety overwhelms and incapacitates. Even this is not too serious if the anxiety is of a short duration such as we might see in stage fright. On other occasions, however, the fear and anxiety persist for long periods of time and the individual feels tense and apprehensive. These emotional reactions activate the body physically to cause trembling, heart-pounding, breathing irregularities, stuttering, constipation, a heavy feeling around the heart and/or a "lump" in the throat. Such symptoms indicate trouble if they last for prolonged periods of time and occur in the absence of any external threat.

*Unusual motor activity*. Sometimes the physical activity of an individual indicates that something is wrong. The following are examples that a church leader might observe:

1. Overactivity. We live in a time and culture in which busyness and persistent activity have become a way of life. But we differ so much in the extent of our activities that what is overactivity for one person may be quite normal behavior for somebody else. For this reason we must know something of the individual's normal pace of life. Overactivity becomes a sign of abnormality when there is a long and persistent speeding up of an individual's typical pace of living. This activity increase may come about for no apparent reason, but it can be seen in the person's verbal, motor, vocational, religious and/or social behavior.

The individual who talks more than he used to, especially if the talking becomes incessant, is showing overactivity in his speech. In a more extreme form, some seriously disturbed perople talk quickly, using real and imagined words in an unintelligible mixture. Motor activity refers to unusual restlessness such as an inability to sit still, a pacing up and down, a constant movement of the hands, feet, eyes or fingers, and/or a jumpiness in response to even slight sounds. Vocational, religious or social overactivity can be seen in a rush from one job to another, from one activity to another, from one meeting to another, and from one party to another. Frequently such people are "always busy" but they never seem to accomplish much.

2. Underactivity. In contrast to overactivity, the under-active individual has slowed down. He may be listless, seemingly tired, and content to do nothing. His speech is slower and talking seems to be an effort. Interest in work, church events or people in general all seems to be minimal.

3. Compulsive activity. A compulsion refers to an irresistible urge to engage in some act, even though this behavior is recognized as being abnormal. In Shakespeare's *Macbeth*, Lady Macbeth compulsively wrung her hands as she walked about following the murder in which she was involved. Often the nature of compulsive activity seems to accomplish nothing, although such habits presumably reduce tension.

Frequent nail-biting, hair-pulling, scratching, eye-blinking, thumb or finger-sucking, masturbation, lip-biting, wringing of the hands, or other ritualistic behavior is often seen in normal people, but in some cases may be indicative of abnormality.

*Disorientation.* The term *orientation* refers to the locating of oneself in time and space. The person who is disoriented does not know where he is, who he is, or what day it is. Such behavior may be rare in a church situation, but occasionally one sees evidence of this in a person who is perplexed and confused, or has periodic blackouts, fainting spells, loss of memory, or other signs of unconsciousness. Since this behavior may result from physical as well as psychological causes, the importance of a physical examination is seen once again.

*Other odd behavior.* There are numerous other psychological signs which are not as common as those listed above but which are, nevertheless, indicators of problems. They include: steady withdrawal from social contacts, increased suspicion of others, a negative attitude toward oneself and others, overresistance to authority, oversubmission to authority, mutism, unusual body movements and grimaces, unexplainable purchases, hiding of objects, speech disturbances, unusual sexual interests or behavior, or a return to childlike behavior.

Again it should be emphasized that such behavior is more likely to indicate abnormality if several signs are apparent at one time, if the behavior represents a change from previous actions, and if the behavior persists.

SOCIAL SIGNS

In listing the psychological indicators of abnormality we made the implicit assumption that the abnormal person acts in ways which are different from the accepted way of life in his society. Kenneth J., for example, wandered "in his back yard at night, praying aloud and shouting that the world was coming to an end." Most people in our culture do not act in this way, but since Kenneth J. does behave like this we conclude that he is different from everybody else and hence abnormal. Abnormality is thus seen here as individual deviation from a society's standards.

Could it be, however, that a whole society or group within a society might be psychologically disturbed? Freud raised this interesting possibility many years ago, [4] and in 1955 a famous psychoanalyst named Erich Fromm published a book in which he suggested that our whole society is "sick." As evidence for this conclusion, Fromm noted that we kill off millions of our population in war; we have an economic system based on the production of armaments; we spend our free time in boredom or being "entertained" by the cheap "trash" of radio, television and movies; and we have high rates of suicide, homicide and alcoholism. To this, Fromm might have added our lowering standards of morality, cutthroat competition to "get ahead," racial strife, reckless driving habits, and a legal system which seems to be degenerating.

According to Fromm,

> The fact that millions of people share the same vices does not make these vices virtues, the fact that they share so many errors does not make the errors to be truths, and the fact that millions of people share the same forms of mental pathology does not make these people sane. [5]

The idea that a whole society can be disturbed is quite consistent with a biblical view of man. All men are sinners who are alienated from God (Ro. 3:23). These alienated men can form societies and live in any way that they choose, but they are still apart from God; their lost condition is seen in their social, political, economic, moral, artistic, intellectual and religious ways of living.

For the church leader who wants to be alert to individual indicators of abnormality, these signs are not of much practical value. For a complete understanding of abnormality, however, we must recognize that society and groups within a society can be and often are psychologically disturbed.

SPIRITUAL SIGNS

As a freshman in college, the author had his first opportunity to visit a mental hospital and was amazed to discover so many evidences of Christianity. Many people talked like Christians, some read their Bibles, there was hymn singing, and the only music on the ward piano was a copy of the same hymnbook that we used in our church. It is not surprising that hospital visitors sometimes conclude that Christianity must in some way be responsible for the condition of mental patients. Many psychologists and psychiatrists seem to have reached the same conclusion and decided that religion is bad for patients.

In some cases, religion *is* bad. If a religious group is "sick" in some way, this could adversely influence the mental

67

stability of its members.* It is more likely that disturbed individuals take basically healthy religious ideas and distort or modify them.[6] The doctor or casual hospital visitor who sees this distorted faith can easily conclude that religion is harmful, but it would be more accurate to decide that as a person's emotion, thinking, perception, orientation and other areas of functioning have been distorted, so too has his religion.

Several types of spiritual behavior can give evidence that something is wrong. It will be noted that the term *spiritual* is used here in a broad sense; perhaps "unusual religious behavior" would be a more accurate title.

*Prolonged guilt feelings.* In chapter 1, guilt was listed as one of the precipitating causes of abnormality. Guilt can also be a symptom of abnormality. Of course, guilt in itself need not be abnormal. Most people feel guilty on occasion and at such times they accept their guilt, confess it, and make restitution. In contrast, pathological guilt is persistent, and the individual will not or cannot accept forgiveness. In his conscious or unconscious mind he is preoccupied with the desires, thoughts or past deeds which make him feel guilty.

*Incapacitating doubts.* The New Testament contains several accounts of doubting by both nonbelievers and believers in Christ. King Agrippa, for example, was "almost persuaded" to be a Christian, but he could not bring himself to accept the gospel message completely (Ac. 26:28). On Mars Hill, Paul found some who believed, but there were others who doubted, laughed at the message, and refused to decide until they could hear more evidence. (Ac. 17:32-34).

---

*Snake-handling cults might be a readily accepted example of a "sick" group. Beyond this, it is difficult to arrive at an acceptable definition of what constitutes abnormality in a group. Some would say that all "fundamentalists" are psychologically abnormal. Others would say Evangelicals should be included. Perhaps even some militant antichurchmen would place all churchmen—including Unitarians and other liberal groups—in the abnormal group.

In the confines of prison, John the Baptist apparently had some doubts and subsequently sent a little delegation to ask Jesus if He really was the Messiah (Mt. 11:1-5). Elsewhere in the Bible we see one of the disciples, who has come to be known as "doubting Thomas," expressing strong doubts that Jesus could come alive after His crucifixion (Jn. 20:25).

In our society, doubting is very common. The high school and college student is encouraged to be skeptical about the things that teachers say in class. The scientist carefully documents his statements because he knows that his scientific colleagues will be doubtful or critical of conclusions that are not supported by good evidence. The textbook writer tries to give reasons for what he says because alert readers will always be ready to challenge any dogmatic statement that is unsupported by logical, scientific or authoritative evidence. Even the preacher, Sunday school teacher or other religious leader can no longer make undocumented statements. The younger and the more educated people in the church are sure to be critical if they do not hear the "reasons why."

There is probably nothing wrong with honest doubting, for the careful asking of questions enables us to find answers and to grow in knowledge. It is interesting to note that Jesus did not condemn John the Baptist or Thomas for their doubting. Instead, He supplied the evidence that met their need. The people of Berea doubted Paul's message, but they searched the Scriptures to see if the apostle was speaking the truth (Ac. 17:11).

In an age which doubts everything, it is not surprising that young people—and older people too—begin to doubt the existence of God, the authority of Scripture, or the wisdom of living a separated life. Rather than stifling these doubts and pretending that they do not exist, many Christian leaders—both within and outside of evangelical churches— are now encouraging young people to openly express their uncertainties and to look for the evidence that will satisfy.

At times, however, this tendency to doubt pervades every area of life. When one doubts the existence of God, the possibility of the supernatural, one's own abilities, or even one's own existence, then there is danger that the individual will become psychologically frustrated or incapacitated. He has faith in nothing and slips into the search for meaning that Frankl describes.[7] This excessive and incapacitating doubt is indicative of the psychological problems of adjustment.

*Fanaticism.* According to the dictionary, fanaticism refers to an "excessive, unreasoning enthusiasm in one's beliefs or behavior, especially in matters having to do with religion." Clearly the Christian should have an intense concern regarding spiritual matters, a life characterized by disciplined periods of prayer and Bible study, and a sincere desire to see others come to know Christ.

Nevertheless, at times such religious zeal is a "cover" for deeper insecurities and psychological problems. Sometimes there is a ritualistic legalism which forgets the believer's freedom in Christ and concludes that Christianity is a set of black and white rules. Those who think in this way are often critical people who make impossible demands upon themselves and others. Other Christians try to maintain a highly emotional "mountaintop" feeling at all times, but their faith is based on much feeling and little fact. Still others live with such a perpetual fear of sinning that their Christian lives are characterized by anxiety, unhappiness and self-condemnation. Eric Sauer summarizes this clearly:

> . . .fanatacism is very often a near neighbor to grave defeat. It makes us self secure, deceives us as to the danger, obscures the vision, and weakens moral determination. The enemy, who narrowly observes all this, will attack quite suddenly, and not seldom very severe defeats, even sins of the flesh, are the open evidence of fanatacism and lack of balance.[8]

It is very difficult to draw a clear line between a healthy religious zeal and religious behavior which covers deeper emotional problems. It should be noted again, however, that it is rarely necessary to rely on only one sign as an indication of abnormality. People with problems express their difficulties in a number of ways; and although religious signs are common, they are only one category of indicators. Table 2-1 summarizes the signs and symptoms of abnormality and could be used as a checklist for spotting problems.

*Table 2-1*

**Signs and Symptoms of Abnormality: A Checklist**

Physical Complaints. . . . . . . . . . . . . . . . . . . . . . . . . . . . . . . . . . . . _____
Psychological Indications. . . . . . . . . . . . . . . . . . . . . . . . . . . . . . . _____
    Frequent Aggression. . . . . . . . . . . . . . . . . . . . . . . . . . . . . . . _____
    Frequent Withdrawal. . . . . . . . . . . . . . . . . . . . . . . . . . . . . . . _____
    Frequent Compromise. . . . . . . . . . . . . . . . . . . . . . . . . . . . . . _____
    Overreliance on Defensive Mechanisms. . . . . . . . . . . . . . . . _____
    Perceptual Difficulties:
        Reduced sensitivity. . . . . . . . . . . . . . . . . . . . . . . . . . . _____
        Increased sensitivity. . . . . . . . . . . . . . . . . . . . . . . . . . _____
        Distorted sensitivity. . . . . . . . . . . . . . . . . . . . . . . . . . _____
        Hallucinations. . . . . . . . . . . . . . . . . . . . . . . . . . . . . . . _____
    Distorted Thinking:
        Nonsensical content. . . . . . . . . . . . . . . . . . . . . . . . . . _____
        Rambling progression of ideas. . . . . . . . . . . . . . . . . . _____
    Faulty Emotional Expression:
        Flat affect. . . . . . . . . . . . . . . . . . . . . . . . . . . . . . . . . . _____
        Elation. . . . . . . . . . . . . . . . . . . . . . . . . . . . . . . . . . . . _____
        Depression. . . . . . . . . . . . . . . . . . . . . . . . . . . . . . . . . _____
        Variability. . . . . . . . . . . . . . . . . . . . . . . . . . . . . . . . . _____
        Inappropriate emotion. . . . . . . . . . . . . . . . . . . . . . . . _____
        Intensive fear and anxiety. . . . . . . . . . . . . . . . . . . . . _____
    Unusual Motor Activity:
        Overactivity. . . . . . . . . . . . . . . . . . . . . . . . . . . . . . . . _____
        Underactivity. . . . . . . . . . . . . . . . . . . . . . . . . . . . . . . _____
        Compulsive activity. . . . . . . . . . . . . . . . . . . . . . . . . . _____
    Disorientation. . . . . . . . . . . . . . . . . . . . . . . . . . . . . . . . . . _____
    Other Odd Behavior. . . . . . . . . . . . . . . . . . . . . . . . . . . . . . _____
Social Signs
Spiritual Indicators:
    Non-Christian. . . . . . . . . . . . . . . . . . . . . . . . . . . . . . . . . . . _____
    Prolonged Guilt Feelings. . . . . . . . . . . . . . . . . . . . . . . . . . . _____
    Incapacitating Doubts. . . . . . . . . . . . . . . . . . . . . . . . . . . . . _____
    Fanatacism. . . . . . . . . . . . . . . . . . . . . . . . . . . . . . . . . . . . . _____

## CLASSIFICATION OF ABNORMALITY

Our discussion in this and the preceding chapter has shown that abnormal behavior can arise from a variety of causes and can be expressed in a number of different ways. So complex are the causes and signs of abnormality that probably no two patients in a mental hospital show exactly the same symptoms or develop a disorder because of identical reasons.

In spite of these wide individual differences, there are, nevertheless, large similarities in patient behavior. Because of this it is possible to categorize people in terms of their most prominent symptoms or in terms of the probable causes of their disorder. Kenneth J., for example, received a diagnosis of *schizophrenia: hebephrenic type*. Probably no other person with this diagnosis is exactly like Kenneth. In spite of this, the diagnostic labels are still used because they summarize the patient's most characteristic behavior, imply something about its causes, and facilitate communication between members of the professional and hospital staff.

Throughout the history of psychiatry, various systems have been used to categorize abnormality. None of these systems has been completely satisfactory and, as more knowledge about deviant behavior is acquired, the existing categorizations are periodically changed and brought up-to-date. In North America, the most widely used system of classification is that proposed by the official diagnostic manual of the American Psychiatric Association. [9]

In Table 2-2 we have summarized the major categories of abnormality and given a brief description of each. The church leader may hear these terms periodically, especially when someone from the congregation is hospitalized. These reactions are described in greater detail in chapters 4 and 5.

## Table 2-2

## Classification of Behavior Disorders*

I. MENTAL RETARDATION. Below normal general intelligence which originates before, during, or shortly after birth and is accompanied by impaired learning, social adjustment, and/or maturation. The term mental retardation is traditionally applied to persons with an I. Q. of less than 70 (about 3 percent of the general population).

II. ORGANIC BRAIN SYNDROMES. Mental disorders which are caused by disease, damage or destruction of brain tissue.
   A. *Psychosis Associated With Organic Brain Syndromes.*
      1. Senile and presenile dementia. Brain disease which results largely from unknown causes and is especially common in the elderly. Major symptoms are childish emotions, self-centeredness, and a difficulty in understanding, accepting or acting on new experiences. Included are Pick's and Alzheimer's diseases.
      2. Alcoholic psychosis. A poisoning of the system by alcohol. Often there are delirium, tremors, hallucinations, memory impairment, jealousy, and distrust of others.
      3. Psychosis associated with intracranial infection. Mental disorders which result from such infections as syphilis, encephalitis, meningitis and brain abscess. All of these affect the nervous system.
      4. Psychosis associated with other cerebral condition. This includes disorders that result from physical influences on the nervous system, other than those described above. Included are cerebral arteriosclerosis (a thickening of the artery walls which results in breakdown of the brain tissue), disturbances in circulation, epilepsy, tumors, diseases which lead to nervous system de-

*Adapted from American Psychiatric Assn., *Diagnostic and Statistical Manual of Mental Disorders,* and E. Rosen and I. Gregory, *Abnormal Psychology,* and W.S. Sahakian, ed., *Psychopathology Today:Experimentation, Theory and Research.*

*Table 2-2 con't*

generation, brain injury and disorders which occur because of brain surgery.

5. Psychosis associated with other physical condition. Included are disorders caused by malfunctioning of glands, malnutrition, infections (such as malaria, pneumonia, typhoid fever, acute rheumatic fever, etc.), poisoning, drug intoxication, childbirth, and other physical conditions.

B. *Nonpsychotic Organic Brain Syndromes.* Sometimes there is something wrong with the brain tissue, but the person is not severely disturbed. He may be easily distracted, impulsive, over or underactive, unresponsive to others or withdrawn, but he is not considered to be mentally ill.

III. PSYCHOSES. These disorders are classified primarily on the basis of symptoms.

A. *Schizophrenia.* A large group of disorders, characterized especially by severe disturbances in thinking, mood and behavior. There are eleven types.

1. Simple type. Apathy, lack of initiative, social withdrawal. No conspicious hallucinations, delusions or intellectual impairment.

2. Hebephrenic type. Shallow and inappropriate affect with hallucinations, delusions, mannerisms, silly and regressive behavior.

3. Catatonic type. Conspicious motor disturbances with inactivity and stupor or excessive activity and excitement.

4. Paranoid type. Poorly systemized (fragmentary and illogical) delusions, usually accompanied by hallucinations. Strong hostility sometimes is expressed in aggressive behavior. The patient thinks he is a very important person (delusions of grandeur) or being plotted against (delusions of persecution).

5. Acute schizophrenic episode. Sudden onset of schizophrenic symptoms, often accompanied by confusion, emotional turmoil, excitement, depression, or fear.

6. Latent type. Patients with clear symptoms of

*Table 2-2 con't.*

schizophrenia but with no past history of the disorder.

7. Residual type. Those who show symptoms for a short time but then show no further schizophrenic behavior.

8. Schizo-affective type. A mixture of schizophrenic symptoms along with pronounced elation or depression.

9. Childhood type. Schizophrenic symptoms which appear before puberty.

10. Chronic undifferentiated type. Prolonged symptoms but with no single type predominating.

11. Other types. Any schizophrenia that cannot be fit into the above categories.

B. *Affective disorders.* A group of disorders characterized either by extreme depression or elation that dominates the behavior and thinking of the individual, causing him to lose contact with his environment.

1. Involutional melancholia. Extreme worry, anxiety, insomnia and/or preoccupations with guilt and physical symptoms. This occurs in the "involutional period"—middle and late middle life—usually in people who have no previous history of psychosis.

2. Manic-depressive behavior. Recurrent episodes of elation or depression, or an alternation between them. Flight of ideas and excitement accompany elation; retardation and inactivity accompany depression. Some people are consistently manic, some are consistently depressed, and some alternate between the two.

C. *Paranoid States.* Disorders in which a delusion of grandeur or persecution is the chief characteristic. Emotion and behavior are consistent with the delusion. Often the delusion proceeds logically from the misinterpretation of some actual event.


IV. NEUROSES. Characterized by consciously experienced anxiety or unconscious attempts to control anxiety by defense mechanisms. Usually there are no gross distortions of reality or disorganization of personality. Neurotics are rarely committed involuntarily to hospitals, but often seek help voluntarily.

*Table 2-2 con't.*

1. Anxiety Neurosis. Persisting anxious overconcern sometimes resulting in panic. Often the anxiety is accompanied by physical indicators of anxiety such as sweating or increased heartbeat.
2. Hysterical Neurosis. An involuntary loss of some aspect of the body's functioning. Psychologically caused blindness, deafness, paralysis, or amnesia are examples. Here the anxiety has been transformed or converted into a physical malfunctioning.
3. Phobic Neurosis. Intense fear of an object or situation which persists despite the individual's realization that the fears are irrational.
4. Obsessive-compulsive Neurosis. A persistent intrusion of unwanted thoughts, urges or actions which the individual is unable to stop.
5. Depressive Neurosis. An excessive reaction of depression due to an internal conflict or the occurence of some disturbing event such as the loss of a loved one or cherished possession.
6. Neurasthenic Neurosis. Chronic fatigue and physical weakness.
7. Depersonalization Neurosis. A feeling of unreality and of being separated from one's body or surroundings.
8. Hypochondriacal Neurosis. A preoccupation with the body and a fear of various diseases.
9. Other Neurosis. This includes a mixture of the above categories.

V. PERSONALITY AND OTHER NONPSYCHOTIC DISORDERS
   A. *Personality Disorders.* Defective personality development or pathological trends in personality. Usually seen in a lifelong pattern of disturbed behavior rather than by disorders of perception, intellectual functions or affect. Anxiety is often not experienced consciously.
      1. Paranoid Personality. A life-style characterized by hypersensitivity, rigidity, unwarranted suspicion, jealousy, envy, excessive feelings of self-importance and a tendency to blame others.
      2. Cyclothymic Personality. A life-style with re-

*Table 2-2 con't.*

curring and alternating periods of depression and elation.

3. Schizoid Personality. A pattern of shyness, over-sensitivity, eccentric behavior, and avoidance of people.

4. Explosive Personality. Excitable people who are periodically given to intense and uncontrollable outbursts of rage and verbal or physical aggressiveness.

5. Obsessive Compulsive Personality. Rigid, over-conscientious people, who are excessively concerned with conformity to standards.

6. Hysterical Personality. Excitable people who overreact to situations, are self-centered, vain, and seeking for attention.

7. Asthenic Personality. A pattern of low energy, lack of enthusiasm, oversensitivity to stress, and easy fatigability.

8. Antisocial Personality. People whose typical behavior is in conflict with society. Such people are intolerant, irresponsible, selfish and apparently unable to learn from experience.

9. Passive-aggressive Personality. This person is aggressive but he expresses his aggression in passive ways such as stubbornness, noncooperation, pouting, intentional inefficiency or cynical remarks.

10. Inadequate Personality. Here the person is consistently inefficient. He shows poor judgement, social instability and inappropriate actions.

B. *Sexual Deviations.* Consistent preference for deviant sexual objects and behavior. This includes homosexuality, transvestism (dressing like the opposite sex), sodism, masochism and voyeurism ("peeping-tom" behavior).

C. *Alcoholism.*

D. *Drug Dependence.*

VI. PSYCHOPHYSIOLOGICAL DISORDERS. These are real physical illness (not just an experience of symptoms) which occur as a result of emotional reactions. Included are psychologically caused ulcers, skin rashes, backaches, bronchial asthma and migraine headaches.

*Table 2-2 con't.*

VII. SPECIAL SYMPTOMS. This category is for the occasional person who shows one single specific symptom such as bed-wetting, speech disturbance, feeding difficulty, sleep disturbance, etc.

VIII. TRANSIENT SITUATIONAL DISTURBANCES. Temporary reactions in persons with basically stable personalities as a response to an overwhelming situation (military combat, civilian catastrophe or other severe environmental stress). May occur in infancy (for example, feeding or sleeping difficulties due to stress), or in any later period.

IX. BEHAVIOR DISORDERS OF CHILDHOOD AND ADOLESCENCE. These are conditions that occur in young people and are more permanent than the transient situational disturbances. Included are youthful overactivity of an excessive nature, anxiety, withdrawal, aggression, or delinquency.

X. OTHER CONDITIONS. This category includes people who are essentially normal but who nevertheless are having severe problems such as marital discord, occupational maladjustment, persistent criminal behavior, or inability to adapt to a new culture.

## COMMON MISCONCEPTIONS

People who have not studied psychology or psychiatry sometimes accept, in good faith, a number of misconceptions about psychological abnormality. Many of these popular but inaccurate ideas have led people to hide their problems and to reject the "mentally ill" whose difficulties are more in the open. Of all people, followers of Christ should be most willing to receive those who are psychologically disturbed; but, to our shame, we too are inclined to reject or fear such people. The church leader is in a key position to counteract misconceptions, to allay fears, to provide information about psychological abnormality, and to encourage the acceptance of all people for whom Christ died.

## ABNORMAL BEHAVIOR ALWAYS RESULTS FROM INDIVIDUAL SIN.

Many Christians believe that the individual who experiences a "nervous breakdown" is living a life which is sinful and not pleasing to God. But if individual sin results in mental illness, then every person who sins (which means everyone) would be at least somewhat abnormal. Abnormality arises from a variety of causes, of which sin is only one. Lest we become proud of our stability and freedom from abnormality, we should remember the words of Jesus when He dealt with the accusers of the woman taken in adultery: "Let him who is without sin cast the first stone." Scripture teaches that all of us sin, and this is *not necessarily* connected with psychological abnormality.

## ABNORMAL BEHAVIOR IS A DISGRACE

People with heart trouble or with other physical problems are respected, accepted and helped in our society, but we still tend to reject those who have psychological disturbances. Many people experience personal problems but are reluctant to seek professional treatment because they know that others look down on the "mentally ill." Sometimes relatives conceal the problems of family members and feel disgraced if hospitalization is necessary. When their treatment is completed, former mental patients often experience difficulty in finding jobs and sometimes are rejected and treated coolly by church members.

Very slowly this attitude is changing. As they learn more about abnormality, people are less afraid and more willing to accept those who have adjustment problems. It should be realized that everyone has a breaking point and that we all face stresses which from time to time make it difficult to function efficiently. Abnormal behavior is unpleasant and unwanted, but it is not a disgrace.

## ABNORMAL BEHAVIOR IS ALWAYS WEIRD AND INCOMPREHENSIBLE

People who have never visited a mental hospital sometimes have the impression that the "inmates. . .spend their time cutting out paper dolls, posing as Napoleon, or ranting and raving." While some patients present this kind of appearance, the majority are well aware of what is going on around them and are able to talk about their problems.

There is no sharp line between behavior which is normal and that which is abnormal. The activities of mental patients differ only in degree from the behavior of more "normal" people, such as the readers of this book. At times, all of us get depressed, disappointed, excited, anxious, worried, awestruck, fearful or elated. If we can imagine one or two of these emotions "taking over" our lives, distorting our perception, coloring our thinking, and influencing our behavior to the extent that we can't get along with others, then we can see that abnormal behavior is really the extreme of that which is normal.

## GENIUS IS AKIN TO MENTAL ILLNESS

Some of the well-known men in history have shown deviant behavior during their lives. Socrates, Democritus, Alexander the Great, King George III of England, Jean Jacques Rousseau, Mozart, Robert Schumann, Vincent van Gogh, Chopin, Schopenhauer, John Stuart Mill, Byron, Burns, Edgar Allen Poe, and more recently, Hitler, Mussolini and Goering are among famous people who reportedly showed evidence of abnormality.

Such reports have led to the conclusion that highly intelligent and creative people, especially those in the arts and sciences, are especially prone to show emotional disturbances. During the past fifty years several studies have shown that this is not so. In the early 1920s, for example, one psychologist tested thousands of California children and selected for further study a group of 1,300 young people who had IQ's of 140 or above. When these gifted children reached adulthood it was found that they had lower mental-illness rates than the general population. (Terman and Oden, 1959). Rather than making people more susceptible to the development of abnormality, therefore, high ability apparently permits them to make better adjustments to life.

## MENTAL ILLNESS IS INCURABLE

A few years ago a ward of the mental hospital was a dead-end street; hospitalization was for life or a long period of time. More recently, with the development of new drugs and treatment techniques, many people have been leaving hospitals permanently after a relatively short stay. Of course, with certain kinds of abnormality (such as severe mental retardation, psychosis associated with severe brain damage, and some senile reactions), significant improvement is rare; but for most patients who receive adequate and early treatment, there is an excellent chance for recovery.

## ABNORMALITY IS INCREASING

Every ten years the population of the United States increases by about 10 percent, but the percent increase in admissions to mental hospitals is much greater, which would seem to indicate that psychological abnormality is on the increase. It is frequently reported that one out of every two hospital beds is now occupied by a mental patient.

Such figures are deceiving, however. As more people have come to accept the view that abnormality is not a disgrace, more have become willing to seek help for their problems. This rise in the numbers seeking help probably represents a change of attitude rather than a change in prevalence of abnormality. Even the statement that half the hospital beds are occupied by mental patients is misleading. Mental patients require longer periods of hospitalization than do other patients, and mental hospitals have a large number of senile elderly people who never leave. Within a given period of time, therefore, a far greater number of people spend time in general hospitals than in mental institutions.

It is difficult to get an accurate estimate of the number of people who, at any given time, are undergoing treatment for behavior problems. For this reason, it is not easy to say whether abnormality is increasing, decreasing or remaining about the same. Of course, regardless of these trends, the problem of psychological abnormality represents a major social issue and a large expense in our society. This should be another reason for concern among church members.

## SUMMARY

Highly unusual behavior is not difficult to recognize, but it is rarely seen by the church leader. The disturbed church member is likely to show more subtle indicators of developing pathology. In this chapter we have described some of these early signs and combined them into a summary checklist which can be used by the church counselor.

Signs of abnormality include physical complaints; psychological malfunctioning such as faulty perception, distorted thinking, unusual motor and physical activity, and strange emotional expressions; social movements; and spiritual indicators such as prolonged feelings of guilt, incapacitating doubts, and fanaticism.

Although each patient shows a different variety of these signs, similar patterns or clusters of symptoms can be recognized. These groups of symptoms can be combined into categories known as syndromes of abnormal behavior. While a formal discussion of these classifications is beyond the scope of this book, the church leader should have at least a casual acquaintance with the "diagnostic categories" that are frequently used in hospitals. These have been listed in a summary table.

Finally, there are some common misconceptions about abnormal behavior which the church should try to counteract. It is incorrect to assume that abnormal behavior always is the result of individual sin, is a disgrace, is always weird and incomprehensible, is especially common in people of genius, is incurable, or is on the increase.

82

# 3

## Assessment and Treatment

Several years ago, 2,460 adults were carefully interviewed about their mental health. Almost one-fifth of these people reported that at some time in life they had felt "on the verge of a nervous breakdown." One in four had experienced a problem for which he felt professional help would have been desirable, and 14 percent of those interviewed had actually sought help for their problems.[1] Probably most of the readers of this book have friends or acquaintances who are currently undergoing treatment for some emotional disturbance, or have had such treatment in the past.

It is not easy to summarize what such treatment is like. Newer treatment and assessment techniques are continually being developed, ongoing research is giving greater insight into the causes of abnormality, and thoughtful professionals are spending many hours trying to find better ways to prevent and to treat abnormal behavior. As a result, new innovations are constantly being tried, and it is possible that treatment techniques may be very different within a few years from what they are now. Already there are geographical differences. A state hospital in Massachusetts, a private clinic in Ontario, and a community mental health center in San Francisco will probably use many of the same assessment and treatment procedures, but they may also differ considerably in some of their approaches.

Concerned about the need for better treatment, the United States Congress provided funds several years ago for a five-year study designed "to analyze and evaluate the needs and resources of the mentally ill in the United States and make recommendations for a National Mental Health Program." [2] The results of this investigation showed a shortage of manpower, facilities and finances, suggested that more money be allotted for mental health research, and proposed some sweeping changes in treatment techniques. It was recommended, for example, that no further state hospitals should be built but that people should be treated in "community mental health centers" or in the psychiatric units of general hospitals. Since there is such a shortage of professional personnel, it was proposed that nonprofessional "mental health workers" should be trained to do "short-term psychotherapy" under the supervision of qualified therapists. These and other recommendations are now being put into practice, but they do not represent any final solution to mental health problems. Clearly more research needs to be done—a conclusion that was also reached by the government committee.

The present chapter gives a brief summary of the techniques which at the present time are most widely used in the *treatment* of disturbed people. Before or during treatment, usually some attempt is made to determine both the nature and the causes of the problem. Some of the *assessment* techniques which are used to provide this information will also be described in this chapter. Since the individual in treatment may come into contact with a number of different trained workers, we will begin by distinguishing between the various mental health professions. The church leader who is familiar with the techniques described in this chapter is better able to communicate with professional counselors, is more comfortable in visiting mental patients, and is better able to minister to families that are concerned about their hospitalized mentally ill relatives.

## MENTAL HEALTH PROFESSIONS

At the present time, several distinct but closely related professions are concerned with the problems of the mentally disturbed. There is considerable overlap in the duties of these professional groups, but there are also differences in training and responsibilities. Because of this, each group brings its own contribution to the "mental health team."

### CLINICAL PSYCHOLOGIST

The clinical psychologist, after four years of college, spends three to five years in graduate school and at least one year as a psychological intern. At the end of his training he receives a PhD degree in clinical psychology and (in most states and provinces) then takes examinations to be certified as a psychologist. Many follow this with one or more years of postdoctoral training.

The clinical psychologist is trained to conduct highly skilled interviews and to engage in individual or group psychotherapy.* Probably his most unique contribution, however, comes in the area of assessment and research. Clinical psychologists are skilled in the administration and interpretation of psychological tests. Since most graduate schools require the clinical student to conduct an experimental research project before he gets his degree, the psychologist also brings to the hospital team a special knowledge of research methodology.

### PSYCHIATRIST

The psychiatrist is a medical doctor. Like all physicians, he must complete four years of college to earn a bachelor's

---

*Not all psychologists are clinical psychologists. Less than half of all who hold doctorates in psychology are trained to work with maladjusted people. The majority of psychologists are involved in teaching, research, personnel work, industrial consultation, and many other noncounseling tasks (A.H. Brayfield, "Psychology as a Profession," *American Psychologist* 23 [ 1968] : 195-200).

degree, four years of medical school after which he receives his MD degree, and a year of internship. He then specializes by taking a psychiatric residency for another three or four years. This residency involves classroom work, study, and supervised contact with psychiatric patients. Following this, he takes examinations in which he is tested on his competence to be a psychiatrist.

In working with the emotionally disturbed, the psychiatrist is especially concerned with diagnosis and treatment. Because of this medical training, he is qualified to prescribe drugs, conduct physical examinations, and use medical techniques in treatment. Like the other mental health specialists, the psychiatrist is a highly trained interviewer who spends much of his time in skillfully conducted psychotherapeutic conversation with his patients.

PSYCHIATRIC SOCIAL WORKER

The psychiatric social worker is especially trained to serve as a link between the patient and his home, and between the hospital and community. The social worker often interviews the family in order to get background information about a patient, helps the family to understand something about the patient's problem, helps the patient to "fit in" when he returns home after treatment, and conducts individual and group therapy sessions.

Like other professionals, the social worker is a skilled interviewer who has a good background in psychology and sociology. His training consists of four years in undergraduate work, usually with a pre-social-work major. This is followed by two years of graduate study leading to a master of social work (MSW) degree. A few psychiatric social workers have doctorates.

PSYCHIATRIC NURSE

The psychiatric nurse is a registered nurse who has taken special additional training in psychology and psychiatry. She specializes in the nursing care of mental patients.

## PSYCHOANALYST

The psychoanalyst is a psychiatrist with several years additional training in the specific techniques of Dr. Sigmund Freud and his followers. Because of the lengthy and specialized preparation, psychoanalysts are relatively rare. Their method of treatment is long and expensive, and for this reason they can accept only a few patients.

## ASSESSMENT

How do professional counselors determine what is wrong with a disturbed individual? Regardless of the place where one seeks treatment, some minimal information will be requested at the beginning: name, address, next of kin, etc. If the person is entering a hospital, he usually has a brief physical examination, is given medication if necessary, and is assigned to a ward. Within a few days, he may be evaluated in some of the following ways (See Figure 1-1, "Assessment").

### PHYSIOLOGICAL DIAGNOSTIC PROCEDURES

A complete physical examination is important in order to determine if physical problems are contributing to the psychological disorder. Hospital patients are always examined by a physician; even when a person is not hospitalized, a complete medical and neurological examination is frequently recommended before treatment begins.

### PSYCHOLOGICAL ASSESSMENT TECHNIQUES

In addition to knowing about the patient's physical state, it is important to be familiar with his psychological symptoms and to uncover, if possible, some of the causes of his psychopathology. This information comes from the patient and from those relatives and friends who know him well. We will look first at the methods which are used to obtain information directly from the patient. The most common of these methods are the interview and psychological tests.

*The interview.* This has been defined, somewhat formally, as "a form of conversation wherein two people, and recently more than two, engage in verbal and non-verbal interaction

for the purpose of accomplishing a previously defined goal." [3]
In the mental hospital or psychological clinic, the goal is to obtain information about the counselee and his problems. To accomplish this the interviewer must be highly skilled in asking questions, stimulating the counselee to talk, and observing nonverbal clues. It is often helpful to find out something about the counselee's current life situation (Is he married? How does he get along with his family? Where does he work? How much education has he had? What are his leisure-time activities and interests?); how he regards his present problem; what life was like before the onset of his problems; and what kinds of difficulties he has had in the past. In addition to what the counselee says, the alert interviewer will watch for such nonverbal clues as squirming, wringing of hands, difficulties in talking, changes in the pitch of the voice, periods of silence, changes in the speed of talking, tears or near tears, inability to answer questions logically, facial grimaces, unusual posture, breathing difficulties, a tendency to change the subject, excessive neatness or sloppiness, and/or inappropriate emotional expression.

The following is a report of information acquired during a thirty-minute interview. By asking penetrating questions and making careful observations, the interviewer was able to learn a great deal about the patient.

Mr. P., a 53-year-old male, is currently hospitalized (in a general hospital) while awaiting heart surgery. His present illness was preceded by consistent good health both for the patient and for the members of the family.

Prior to the onset of his illness, Mr. P. worked in a department store, assisted his two sons in their activities in the minor league, held a position in his church, and spent most of his leisure time with the immediate family. The patient clearly appears to have been head of the household — and to have seen himself as such — but he was not overly domineering in this role. The sons, for example, were left pretty much on their own to play as they wished (within the bounds of some broad limits). Mrs. P. was welcome to accompany her husband and the boys on their family camping trips if she so desired, but she could also decide to remain at home without upsetting the rest of the family.

When the illness occurred, the family met a novel crisis but apparently the ensuing period of disruption was fairly smooth. Mrs. P. took over the functions of running the household and the sons did much of the work at home such as mowing the lawn.

In spite of the somewhat blasé manner in which Mr. P. described these family changes, he was very much involved emotionally. The perpetual movement of his foot during the interview and the periodic inappropriate smiling gave some indication of his tension, as did the periods when he would wipe away a tear or find it difficult to verbalize his feelings. At such times, his jaw would move as if he were trying to speak but first wanted to be certain that he "had control." After he was offered a kleenex (which at first he refused), he appeared to be a little less determined to hold back his tears. The tears appeared to come when the interviewer focused on the patient's illness or his altered family situation. When he described his boys, talked of the coming operation, mentioned the possibility that he might not recover, or talked about things which he could no longer eat, he appeared to be the most upset. Part of this emotional reaction may have been influenced, however, by the fact that this was the first occasion in which Mr. P. had been able to discuss the emotional aspects of his illness with anyone.

In summary, it would appear that Mr. P. is meeting the first real sickness in his family by discussing his feelings with no one (probably because there is no one with whom he can talk). As he approaches surgery for the first time, he sees that his family apparently can get along by themselves. It is possible that he is disturbed not only by fear of the coming surgery but also by loss of his status as head of the family.

While the interview is probably the oldest and most commonly used of the information-gathering techniques, studies have shown that this procedure is not very valid.[4] Since an interviewer can't observe everything, he tends to be selective in his perceptions. When one patient is interviewed by two different people, for example, the interviewers often notice different behaviors. This problem of interview validity is worsened when the patient is uncooperative or wants to be deceptive. On such occasions, even the most skilled interviewers are sometimes fooled. Because of this, the interview is often supplemented with information gathered by other techniques.

*Psychological tests.* These are valuable tools for providing this additional information. An interviewer does not ask everyone the same questions. Instead, he asks different questions of different persons, makes his observations, and then tries to assimilate his information into some kind of meaningful conclusion. In contrast, the psychological tester is much more systematic. He asks the same questions of everyone. Then he compares an individual's responses with the *norms* or answers that have been given when the questions were asked previously of hundreds of other people.

As an example of testing design, let us suppose that the following is a question on some psychological test: "Do you worry about things so that you can't sleep at night?" Let us suppose, further, that this question had been previously presented to 1,000 normal people and to 1,000 hospitalized mental patients. We might discover that the normal people and the patients answer the question quite differently. If this question is now given to a specific patient who has come to a hospital or clinic, we can look at his answer, compare it with the answers of the normal people and patients, and thus get an idea of where our respondent stands in comparison to these two groups. The psychological test, of course, is composed of many questions, but for each question the test designer finds out how normal and abnormal people would answer. Once we have this information, we can more accurately evaluate the responses given by any one individual.

There are literally hundreds of psychological tests. Many, including most of those described in this chapter, have been carefully designed and appear to be accurate indicators of behavior. Others, including almost all of those that appear in popular magazines or in the Sunday papers, are poorly designed and of no real value. Fortunately, competent designers of tests have set up some rigid standards in an attempt to improve the quality of test construction. [5]

Psychological assessment techniques are of three main types: systematic observation, self-report techniques, and performance tests.

1. Systematic observation. In our discussion of the interview we emphasized the importance of watching behavior. This observation is easier and more accurate when done systematically rather than in a hit-and-miss fashion. Of the systematic observation techniques, probably the rating scale is most commonly used.

If a Sunday school superintendent wanted to evaluate teachers, he could watch them casually to see how they performed. But the superintendent's observations could be more systematic and hence more accurate if he used a rating scale similar to that shown in Figure 3-1. Perhaps he could also have students give their ratings of the teacher. By using a device such as this, it also would be possible to systematically compare one teacher's performance with that of another.

In psychological treatment centers, a rating scale is sometimes used by a psychologist or a psychiatrist who completes it as he conducts an interview, or by nurses and aids who are in a position to observe the patient's behavior on the ward.

Of course, this technique is less accurate if the rater has a bias (either in favor of or against the person being rated). If several raters observe one person, however, and if the raters are alert to this biasing tendency, the rating procedure can often yield accurate and valuable information.

*Figure 3-1*

## Sample Rating Scale for Evaluation of Sunday School Teachers*

**For each of the characteristics listed below, circle the response that most accurately describes the teacher.**

1. The presentation of the subject matter is
   A. Very clear
   B. Fairly clear
   C. Somewhat clear
   D. Not very clear
   E. Not at all clear

2. In relating to his students, the teacher is
   A. Very friendly
   B. Fairly friendly
   C. Somewhat friendly
   D. Not very friendly
   E. Not at all friendly

3. The teacher gives the impression of being
   A. Always prepared
   B. Usually prepared
   C. Sometimes prepared
   D. Rarely prepared
   E. Never prepared

4. The teacher is
   A. Always on time
   B. Usually on time
   C. Sometimes on time
   D. Rarely on time
   E. Never on time

5. When members of his class are absent without explanation, the teacher contacts the absentees.
   A. Always
   B. Usually
   C. Sometimes
   D. Rarely
   E. Never

2. Self-report technique. Sometimes the person being tested is asked to rate himself. His responses are then compared with the responses of other people, some of whom show abnormal behavior. These self-report techniques usually take the form of paper-and-pencil tests and include the following:

*a.* Sentence completion tests. In this test the individual is given a few words and asked to complete the sentence in a way that expresses his real feelings. Examples of sentence stems include: "I like . . .," "I hate . . .," "Sex is . . .," "I can't . . .," "I secretly . . .," and "My greatest fear . . . ."

*b.* Checklists. Here a list of adjectives (e.g., happy, depressed, bored with life, persistent, etc.) is presented, with the respondent checking those traits that describe himself. In a variation of this procedure, the Mooney Problem Checklist presents 330 problems and the person taking the test checks those items that describe his own difficulties.[6] Problems include the following:

> Feeling tired much of the time.
> Having beliefs that differ from my church.
> Failing to see the relation of religion to life.
> Awkward in meeting people.
> Being too envious or jealous.
> Having a troubled or guilty conscience.
> Not reaching the goal I've set for myself.

*c.* Questionaires and inventories. Here the respondent either answers a number of written questions about himself or he reads a statement and indicates whether this is true of him or not true. Probably the best-known inventory is the Minnesota Multiphasic Personality Inventory, usually abbreviated as MMPI. This consists of over 500 statements, including the following:

93

I believe I am being followed.
Often I can't understand why I have been so cross and grouchy
At times I feel like smashing things.
I am entirely self-confident.
I am afraid of using a knife or anything very sharp or pointed.
My daily life is full of things that keep me interested.

To each of these questions the test-taker responds "true," "false," or "cannot say." These responses are then tallied and compared with the answers given by mental patients whose behavior has caused them to be grouped into the major diagnostic categories. Thus, the psychologist can see if the respondent marks the items in the same way that they are answered by schizophrenics, paranoids, hypochondriacs, manics, or other types of patients. This test not only indicates tendencies in the direction of abnormality, but it has a built-in device which tells whether the respondent is lying or otherwise distorting the results.

3. Performance tests. A large number of tests require the respondent to react with some kind of behavior. Unlike the self-report techniques which the individual pretty much takes on his own, performance tests are usually administered by psychologists to one person at a time. In evaluating the psychological functioning of mental patients, the most commonly used performance techniques are intelligence tests, projective tests, and brain-damage tests.

   *a.* Intelligence tests. Intelligence can be measured in a number of ways. The so-called paper-and-pencil tests which are given to military recruits or to groups of schoolchildren provide an acceptable indication of general intellectual ability. In assessing abnormality, however, these tests are of little practical use. More widely used in clinical situations are devices like the Stanford-Binet-Intelligence Scale, the Wechsler Intelligence Scale for Children (WISC), and the Wechsler Adult Intelligence Scale (WAIS). The first two of these are used with children while the third, as the name indicates, is an adult test. In each of these a skilled tester presents materials that require verbal or nonverbal answers. In the WAIS, for example, the subject may be asked to define a number of words, indicate how praise and punishment are alike, repeat a list of digits without error, do mental arithmetic, arrange scrambled pictures into a logical sequence, indicate what is missing in a number of incomplete pictures, assemble jigsaw puzzle pieces, or answer questions like "What is the Apocrypha?"

From the test-taker's responses to items such as these, it is possible to determine the intelligence quotient, or IQ, which is an indication of the respondent's current level of intellectual functioning. But these tests also can be used to determine brain damage, to check for changes in intellectual performance (which often comes with emotional disturbances), or to observe distorted thinking. As he administers the test the psychologist is able to observe anxiety, indecision, reaction to failure, ability (or inability) to concentrate, and other behavior. Since any one test is always administered according to rigid requirements, the tester is able to compare the behavior of each respondent with that of many others who have been in a similar test-taking situation.

*b.* Projective tests. In these tests, the individual is presented with a vague and ambiguous stimulus, like a picture of an inkblot, and asked to tell what he sees. It is assumed that in giving his answer the respondent will "project" or show forth a lot of his conflicts and thinking.

Probably the most widely used projective device is an inkblot test which was designed many years ago by a Swiss psychiatrist named Herman Rorschach. Ten inkblots, similar to that shown in Figure 3-2, are presented to the respondent, who is asked to tell what he sees. The psychologist makes note of what is seen, the parts of the blot that are used, and whether or not the subject sees shading, movement, color or texture. From this it is possible to get an indication of the nature and extent of the respondent's abnormality.

The Thematic Apperception Test (TAT) is composed of a number of pictures. The respondent looks at each picture and is expected to make up a story about what he sees. The following story was given by a patient in response to a picture of a young boy sitting at a table and looking at a violin:

> He's sitting there because he broke his fiddle. He is acting real mad about it. He must have been playing or something like that, and he broke it. He is just sitting at the table looking at it. I guess it was his. He is mad. One of his friends may have broken it, and he is going to call his mother and tell her what happened. I guess his mother will straighten things out. Maybe she will buy him a new one.

In analyzing this response, one psychologist concluded that the story

> reveals at least five themes. First there is the idea of the "broken fiddle", suggesting hostility and aggression. Second, the patient telling the story says twice that the boy is "mad" about it, emphasizing feelings of anger. The third theme is a possible paranoid one derived from the statement that "one of his friends may have broken it". Maternal dependency is suggested by the fact that the boy is going to "call his mother". The fifth theme is optimism and is expressed by the fact that the mother probably will "straighten things out" and "buy him a new one." [7]

The reader may wonder how the psychologist in the above example was able to arrive at so many conclusions on the basis of this one story. To a large extent, his training teaches him what to look for and how to interpret a patient's responses. But projective tests bring forth a great variety of responses. It is very difficult to collect norms showing how "most people respond," and, as a result, trained testers sometimes come up with different interpretations. For this reason some psychologists question the value of these tests; but like all assessment techniques, projective measures must be used and interpreted in conjunction with other data.

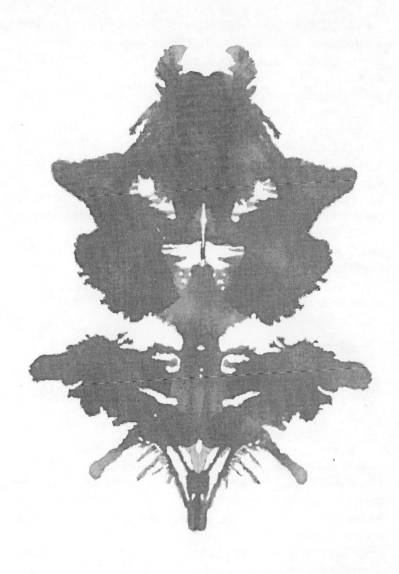

*Figure 3-2*

**Inkblot similar to those of the Rorschach Test**

In addition to the Rorschach and TAT, projective testing includes analysis of the patient's drawings, play, handwriting, finger painting, and performance in dramatic "role play" situations.

*c.* Brain-damage tests. When the brain is injured or deteriorating, psychological functioning is likely to be impaired in some way. While this impairment is sometimes difficult to detect, even with neurological procedures, there are psychological tests which can indicate when something is wrong with the brain. Most of the brain-damage tests measure perceptual-motor behavior. This means that the respondent must look at some stimulus and make a response. In the Graham-Kendall Memory-for-Designs Test, for example, a design similar to Figure 3-3 is shown.[8] After ten seconds the figure is removed and the respondent is required to draw this from memory. When compared with normals, brain-damaged people have greater difficulty in reproducing such figures.

SOCIOLOGICAL ASSESSMENT

As noted in chapter 1, behavior is determined, in a large measure, by one's social environment. The interview and psychological testing will probably reveal something about this background, but it is also helpful to talk with people who are well-acquainted with the patient.

The psychiatric social worker, with his training in sociological techniques, is especially equipped to make this investigation. Often he is in a good position to ask about the patient's behavior before treatment, to make observations about the patient's family, and to visit the patient's home and neighborhood. Sometimes a questionnaire or rating scale may be used in this investigation, but more often information is acquired through interviews.

Of course, it should not be assumed that the psychiatric social worker is the only professional person that a patient's family will see. Psychologists, psychiatrists and others also appreciate the opportunity to talk with the family members.

In previous chapters we have suggested that spiritual factors can play an important part in the development of abnormality and that there are spiritual signs which indicate maladjustment. If this is so, then it seems logical that the pastor or hospital chaplain could give considerable help to the professional team as they try to determine what is wrong with a disturbed individual. The pastor is in a unique position to understand the nature of religious conflicts and to appreciate the meaning of some of the spiritual indications of abnormality. Several writers have recently suggested that an interview conducted by a chaplain and dealing primarily with the patient's religious life, could reveal helpful information which other members of the assessment team might miss.[9]

Regretfully, there are relatively few treatment centers at present that include a chaplain on the assessment team. Hopefully this type of pastoral ministry will become more prevalent in the future as the attitudes of hospital personnel change and as additional seminary students are trained for this significant kind of work.

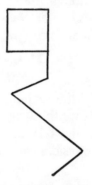

*Figure 3-3*

**Design similar to those of the Graham-Kendall Memory-for-Designs Test**

## STAFF CONFERENCE

By observing a patient for a few days and talking with his family, the various members of the hospital staff are able to accumulate a large amount of information. This information is frequently discussed at a meeting where everyone who has seen the patient or who might be expected to work with him, meets together to decide on a treatment plan. Some of the common treatment procedures are described in the next section.

At this point it should be emphasized that use of the assessment procedures which we have been describing, and treatment with the techniques which will be discussed below are characteristic of ideal situations only. Many treatment centers are understaffed, and the professional personnel are overburdened. In such situations, the existing personnel must "fill in" as best they can, but often this results in poor patient care.

## TREATMENT

The type of treatment that is used in a given situation depends on the nature of the disturbance, on the type of treatment center, and on the training or theoretical position of the therapist.* Although there is considerable overlap, treatment techniques can be classified as primarily medical, psychological, social or spiritual.

### MEDICAL TREATMENT PROCEDURES

The psychiatrist or other medically trained therapist may choose to use any of the techniques which are common in modern medicine. If we think again of the biological causes of abnormality (see Fig. 1-1), it is obvious that a change of diet, a program of physical exercise, medication to correct

---

*The therapist is defined as one who is "skilled in the employment of treatment techniques" (H. B. English and Ava C. English, *A Comprehensive Dictionary of Psychological and Psychoanalytical Terms*, p. 551). This may be a clinical psychologist, psychiatrist, psychiatric social worker or other trained counselor.

a glandular dysfunction, plastic surgery to change some embarrassing facial feature, or a host of other strictly medical procedures can have a profound influence on behavior. In addition, some medical techniques are especially useful in the treatment of patients with psychiatric problems. These techniques include drug therapy, shock therapy, and psychosurgery.

*Drug therapy.* Throughout history, men have used drugs to "dim the unpleasantness of everyday life." Stone age people used opium, the Egyptians drank wine, and for centuries people all over the world have used herbs and roots as sedatives.[10] After the Second World War, when drugs became widely used in the treatment of abnormality, there were dramatic changes in patient behavior. There was less agitation, more cooperation, and a marked reduction in the length of hospital stay. Today, as is well known, a large variety of drugs are used in psychiatric treatment, and new medications are frequently making their appearance.

The most widely used of these drugs can be classified into two main categories. *Tranquilizers* reduce anxiety and calm down the individual so that he feels less tense and more relaxed but still able to think clearly. *Antidepressants* are drugs which energize patients who are apathetic, lethargic and depressed. These drugs stimulate the individual so that he feels "brighter," less discouraged, and more willing to interact with other people.

While drugs can change behavior and reduce extreme symptoms, they should not be thought of as a cure-all. Mental disorders caused by severe stress, strong guilt feelings, or early family turmoil, for example, can hardly be cleared up with a few pills. The tranquilizers and antidepressants temporarily mask symptoms, suppress abnormal behavior, and make the individual more able to grapple with his problems under the guidance of a professional counselor. To bring permanent behavior change, however, drugs must be used along with other methods of treatment.

101

*Shock therapy.* This type of treatment also has a long history. The ancient methods of dunking people in ice water or burning them with hot irons were certainly shock-inducing techniques. In contrast, modern shock treatment is humane, painless, and often very effective in alleviating the symptoms of depressed people (especially those who are elderly) and some schizophrenics. Nobody really knows why shock treatments are effective, although a number of people have made guesses.

The two most commonly used shock therapies are insulin shock and electroshock. With *insulin shock therapy* the patient is given an injection of insulin which changes the level of sugar in the blood, resulting in unconsciousness and convulsions, followed by a coma. When the patient "wakes up" he is more rational, more sociable, less withdrawn, and better able to participate in other forms of therapy.

*Electroshock therapy* is more widely known. In this procedure, the patient lies on his back on a well-padded bed. A rubber gag is placed in his mouth, and a drug is injected to relax the muscles and reduce the danger of bone fractures or dislocations. Electrodes are placed on his temples, and for a fraction of a second a current of 100 to 200 volts is passed through his head. The patient, who feels no pain, loses consciousness immediately, becomes rigid for about 10 seconds, and then begins jerky convulsions. During this time, attendants hold his shoulder and limbs lightly to prevent him from falling off the bed or otherwise injuring himself. After about thirty seconds the convulsions stop, the patient sleeps, and within the next half hour he wakes up. At first he is drowsy and confused, but soon he feels better and has no memory of the shock or convulsions.

With the widespread development of antidepressant drugs, shock therapy is now used less frequently. Many psychiatrists still feel that it is effective, however, especially with patients who do not respond to drugs, but others have expressed a concern that this technique can cause minor brain damage.

*Psychosurgery.* This is a brain operation in which the surgeon cuts some of the nerve pathways in the brain. Sometimes portions of the brain are even removed or purposely destroyed. This, of course, is a very extreme type of therapy and is used only when everything else fails. As drugs have come into greater use, psychosurgery is being used less and less, until today this procedure is relatively rare.

## PSYCHOLOGICAL TREATMENT TECHNIQUES

Whenever we have problems it is often helpful if we can talk things over with another person. Simply stated, psychotherapy is a form of psychological treatment in which a problem is talked over by a disturbed individual and a highly skilled counselor. The person with the problem is usually called the patient, client, or counselee, while the counselor is at times referred to as a psychotherapist or, more simply, a therapist.

The goals of psychotherapy vary somewhat with the nature of the counselee's problem and the theoretical views of the therapist. Sometimes these goals are very clear; sometimes they are vague. But, in general, psychotherapy usually attempts to achieve one or more of the following: (1) increasing insight by the counselee into the nature and causes of his problems and behavior; (2) a clearer awareness of one's self-identity (that is, an increased ability to answer such questions as "Who am I?" or "What are my goals in life?"); (3) a resolution of handicapping conflicts; (4) a changing of undesirable habits or ways of behavior; (5) improved ability to get along with other people; (6) a change in the perception of oneself and others; and (7) a more meaningful and satisfying life.[11] To this list we might add (8) a decreased need to rely on incapacitating symptoms, and (9) an overcoming of one's separation from God.

This impressive list of goals is very difficult to obtain. To reach them, the therapist at times may use reassurance,

suggestions, advice, reasoning, persuasion, or other moti-
vational techniques. [12] Therapy may encourage and support
the counselee's present behavior or it may completely change
the personality. The process may be brief, lasting for one
or two sessions, or it may continue for several years. Furthermore, the therapist may work with one counselee at a time
(individual therapy), or with several (group therapy). Sometimes the counselee is seen both individually and in a group.

*Individual therapy.* For best results, individual therapy
must be characterized by a warm personal relationship between the therapist and his client. When this relationship
is established, therapists proceed in different ways although
most rely on the treatment techniques that have been suggested by the different schools of therapy. Of these, psychoanalysis, client-centered therapy, behavior therapy, and (to
a much lesser extent) logotherapy are among the more widely used.

Psychoanalysis is based on the theories and techniques of
Sigmund Freud. Although Freud's followers have largely
modified his techniques, the basic approach is for the patient to be on a couch where he "free associates," which
means that he says whatever comes to mind. The therapist
"interprets" the meaning of this talk and seeks to develop
insight in his patient. This is an expensive treatment technique which usually continues for several years and attempts
to completely restructure the personality.

Client-centered (or nondirective) therapy assumes that
man is quite capable of solving his own problems. The therapist, therefore, listens to his client talk, accepts the client's
thoughts and feelings without criticism or interpretation,
summarizes them, and makes statements which "reflect
the client's feelings." The client-centered therapist never
tells the client what is causing the problems or how they can
be solved. In this respect the therapy is nondirective—the
responsibility for change depends on the client, not on the
therapist. Hopefully the counselee feels so comfortable

and accepted in the counseling situation that he can openly recognize his feelings, gain insight into the sources of his problem, and make his own plans for changing behavior.

Obviously this technique, which was developed by psychologist Carl Rogers, does not work very well with disorientated psychotics. It has been effective, however, with college students and other intellectually capable young people who experience marriage and vocational problems, adjustment problems, or mild forms of neurosis.

Behavior (learning) therapy is based on the assumption that all behavior—including abnormal behavior—is learned. The therapist becomes a teacher who might use any number of learning techniques to eliminate undesirable ways of acting and to bring about more appropriate behavior. This type of therapy is comparatively new but has been used with apparent success in the treatment of a wide variety of disorders.[13]

Logotherapy is the procedure that Frankl has developed.[14] The therapist confronts the counselor with his lack of direction in life, and subsequently the person in treatment is helped to find meaning. There is no attempt to force the therapists' values on the counselee. Instead, it is assumed that the specific meaning of life differs from person to person and that therapy will help the counselee to "find" his own meaning.

*Group therapy.* Sometimes a therapist will meet with several troubled people at the same time. The group members discuss their own problems and feelings with each other while the therapist encourages conversation, keeps the topic from wandering too far from its original point, reflects group or individual attitudes and feelings, and sometimes makes suggestions or interpretations.

The group member frequently is helped by realizing that others have problems similar to his. Often the group gives emotional support to an individual and helps him to learn what behavior is socially appropriate. There is real value in seeing ourselves as others see us, and the group provides this experience. In a sense, then, every group member is a therapist for every other.

*Other psychological treatment techniques.* Sometimes family therapy will be part of a treatment plan. This is a special form of therapy in which the group consists of two or more members of the same family. Hypnotherapy is a procedure in which the patient is hypnotized so that the therapist is able to deal with issues which are normally hidden in the unconscious. Psychodrama takes place on a stage where the patient, his therapist, and one or two other people act out fears, conflicts, or interpersonal situations. Recently marathon groups lasting for twenty hours or more, and sometimes conducted with all participants in the nude, have been advocated as an effective therapeutic device.[15]

ENVIRONMENTAL MODIFICATION

To this point we have assumed that therapeutic efforts must always be geared toward directly changing the counselee, but there is another way to alter behavior. Often abnormalities will disappear if the client's environment can be changed. This modification of the environment is known as sociotherapy or milieu therapy—a treatment technique which most often is used along with individual psychotherapy.

Sometimes the hospital atmosphere is so much less stressful than the home situation that the patient improves almost as soon as he is admitted. If, following hospitalization, this patient has to return to the same old stresses at home, the influence of treatment will not last very long. In order to prevent this "hospital relapse," milieu therapy uses two techniques.

First the hospital is made as much like the "outside society" as possible. Employees often wear street clothes instead of uniforms, the patients and staff members work and eat together, there is an elected ward council to plan recreation or hear grievances, and there is a minimum of locked doors

106

and patient restrictions. By making the hospital less like an institution and more like a community, patients can learn how to react appropriately in relatively normal situations. When the time comes to be discharged from the hospital, there is not an abrupt change as one moves back into the society.

Second, an attempt is often made to change the home situation. Social workers and community agencies work with the patient's family to reduce the home pressures and resolve some of the family conflicts. With the eventual elimination of big mental hospitals and the centering of treatment in the patient's community, hopefully these environmental factors can be more easily controlled.

In addition to milieu therapy, other social techniques include playing or listening to music, painting, reading, or taking part in social events and athletic programs. Many patients are also encouraged to take part in occupational therapy which consists of crafts, hobbies, and constructive work within the hospital.

SPIRITUAL THERAPY

Do the foregoing techniques help a person who is alienated from God and spiritually distressed? With the possible exception of logotherapy and some other forms of psychotherapy, most treatment techniques ignore man's spiritual needs. Indeed, the majority of therapists probably would agree that psychotherapy and religious counseling have little bearing on one another. Many feel that the therapist who uses scientific procedures to deal with behavior disturbances has neither the competence nor the interest in dealing with religious experiences and beliefs.

In contrast to this view, Dr. Donald Tweedie, a Christian psychologist in California, has noted that at least some persons see no necessary incompatability between these two areas. "Their thesis is that psychotherapy must not be neutral to the Christian faith. . . . They demand, rather, a psychotherapy founded on Biblical presuppositions."16

But professionally qualified Christian therapists such as these are rare! Most church members who seek treatment are likely to encounter a therapist who has a limited understanding of spiritual matters and little personal interest in religion. Such nonbelieving psychologists or psychiatrists can be ot help to Christians, especially when the problem has little to do with one's spiritual condition. In many—perhaps most—situations, however, the emotional disturbance *does* have spiritual implications. The non-Christian professional worker may show a sympathetic attitude toward religion, but he is really unable to understand the believer's way of looking at the world. In addition, the therapist's personal values and beliefs have been shown to influence counseling. Thus, the nonbeliever may have difficulty in dealing effectively with some of the problems and conflicts that a Christian faces. When no Christian therapist is available, therefore, the pastor (or some other church leader) often seeks to cooperate with the therapist in the treatment plan. In some cases, the church leader can be a more effective counselor than the non-believing therapist.

Unfortunately, as Mowrer has pointed out, many church leaders have recently become so impressed with secular psychotherapy that they have forgotten about their own spiritual resources.[17] Clergymen and other well-meaning church members have neglected their theological knowledge and have tried instead—largely without success—to become miniature copies of nonbelieving therapists.

To help disturbed people with their spiritual and other problems, the Christian counselor must be a devoted follower of Christ, a student of the Bible, and an individual who has had training in counseling techniques. While the Christian psychotherapist has the best preparation for this ministry, the consecrated church leader who is trained in counseling procedures can also be effective in helping disturbed people with their problems.

## PSYCHOTHERAPY AND VALUES

For many years, therapists and counselors were taught that their own beliefs and values should be carefully hidden during an interview. It was assumed that in talking with a counselee, successful therapists showed no feelings and expressed no value judgments.

We now know that such counselor neutrality is impossible. "If a person interacts in any way with another person, he is going to disseminate values," wrote one therapist. "So we might as well be explicit about it, admit it, and think about it."[18] When careful studies were made of interviews, it was found that a therapist could express his own reactions and manipulate the behavior of a counselee by such simple mannerisms as a slight head nod, a few "uh-huh" responses or changes in his facial expression.[19] In view of these and other studies, it has become apparent that we cannot act without revealing our own values. Implicitly or explicitly, the counselor's ethics, values and philosophy influence and even determine the goals of therapy. It follows that counselor values will also influence the methods and techniques which are means toward these goals.

Clearly the time has come for therapists to be aware of their beliefs and, on occasion, to openly express them in counseling. "As psychologists familiarize themselves with the value orientation under which they operate," Lowe has written, they should "confess their philosophical biases and then turn these biases to fullest advantage by being of professional assistance to the special interest groups with which their values coincide."[20] This would suggest that, whenever possible, evangelical counselees should consult evangelical therapists, Catholics should choose Catholics, and atheists should choose counselors who are nonbelievers.

Several years ago, when the author was employed in the counseling center of a state university, it was found that many students were searching for a system of values and a purpose in life. On several occasions, rather than attempting to re-

109

main neutral, I shared with these students the value system which was meaningful to me as a Christian. In my opinion this was not "pushing religion," but was the sharing of a system which sometimes explicitly and sometimes implicitly guides all of my counseling. On other occasions I have counseled with students who have left the church and rejected their evangelical upbringing. In accepting their decision to reject the church, I have nevertheless informed them of my own Christian commitment. This is simply being honest, and honesty is the basis of all effective communication.

## EFFECTIVENESS OF TREATMENT TECHNIQUES

As we have examined the different methods of treatment in this chapter, some readers may have wondered about the effectiveness of these techniques. Do they all work to alleviate the suffering of emotionally disturbed people? Advocates of different treatment techniques often will point to one or two individual examples of dramatic improvement, but these case histories prove nothing! Every therapist can find a few successes, some of which may have occurred spontaneously or in spite of (rather than because of) the treatment. Clearly, if we are to demonstrate the value of any treatment technique, we must conduct carefully designed research studies.

During the past thirty years a number of these studies have been conducted. Although the results are contradictory and somewhat difficult to summarize, it appears that the different techniques—and especially psychotherapy—are much less effective than we would like to think.[21] Dr. Hans Eysenck, a well-known and controversial British psychologist, has convincingly argued that the effects of psychotherapy are very small.[22] On this side of the Atlantic, Dr. Paul Meehl, former president of the American Psychological Association, has estimated that only one in four patients is likely to benefit greatly from therapy and that only one in four therapists is really good in his job. This would suggest that there is only one chance in sixteen of a suitable patient getting to a suitable therapist.[23]

These rather pessimistic conclusions are not likely to convince professional counselors or the thousands of people who believe that treatment has helped. Indeed, there is some evidence to suggest that when the counselee and therapist expect that therapy will work, it does! In time, research techniques will improve and we will get a better understanding both of abnormal behavior and of those methods of treatment which are most effective. Until then, it is probably most accurate to say that *every type of treatment helps some patients.* If one procedure does not work with a given individual, then it is likely that some other treatment will be effective.

## SUMMARY

The church leader should have some understanding of what goes on in mental hospitals or other treatment centers. Such knowledge makes it easier to communicate with professional people and to minister to the patients and their families.

Among the professional people who work with the emotionally disturbed are clinical psychologists, psychiatrists, psychiatric social workers, psychiatric nurses, and psychoanalysts. These professional people use a variety of techniques and work in a number of different treatment centers. In most cases an attempt is made to understand something about the patient's problem. To do this, a number of assessment techniques are used, including the physician's well-known diagnostic procedures, psychological techniques such as interview and testing, and sociological investigations of the patient's home background. Treatment techniques include drug therapy, shock therapy, individual psychotherapy, group therapy, environmental modification, and spiritual counseling. In many of these, the therapist's own beliefs and values are important and influential. While all of these techniques appear to be useful with at least some

111

people, it is clear that assessment and treatment could still be much more effective. For this reason, experimentation with new procedures and research into the effectiveness of older procedures is continuing.

# 4

## Common Abnormal Reactions

In the past three chapters we have been discussing abnormal behavior in general, but apart from Table 2-2, little attempt has been made to deal with the specific diagnostic categories or *syndromes* of abnormality. It is to these that we now turn.

In doing this it might be wise to consider why any of this should concern the church leader. Why can't he overlook terms like "hebephrenic schizophrenia" or "hysterical neurosis" and leave the technical jargon for the specialists? It is hardly necessary for the pastor or other church worker to have an exhaustive knowledge of abnormal psychology, but if he is familiar at least with the more common terms he can better *detect* problems in their early stages of development, he can *understand* the patient's condition and behavior if the problem becomes severe, and he can more effectively *counsel* with the patient and his family.

In this chapter we do not attempt to summarize all of the mental disorders. Instead we have selected those which seem most likely to be encountered by the church leader. Some of the diagnostic categories from Table 2-2—such as mental retardation or marital maladjustment—are not mentioned in this chapter because they are discussed elsewhere in the Psychology for Church Leaders series. For most of the disorders that are considered we will describe the most characteristic signs and symptoms, indicate the assumed causes, summarize the treatment techniques that are most often used with each, and then indicate the likelihood of recovery.

## ORGANIC BRAIN DISORDERS

When a part of the brain is diseased, damaged or destroyed, there are often changes in behavior. The most common of these are confusion, problems with memory, difficulties in learning and comprehension, poor judgment, inappropriate emotional expression, and deterioration in appearance or moral standards. These behavior changes can sometimes be spotted by the church leader who, by persuading the parishioner to get a medical checkup, can thereby help to arrest a serious illness.

Brain disorders may result from a variety of causes. These include infections such as meningitis, encephalitis, or syphilis (a disease in which the brain or other internal organs may, over a period of years, be "eaten away"), head injuries, brain tumors, or poisoning from drugs and fumes. In older people, brain disorders sometimes occur because the blood supply to the brain is slowly blocked by arteriosclerosis— a hardening and thickening of the blood vessel walls. Sometimes the blood flow is stopped suddenly because an artery ruptures or a clot interferes with the movement of blood to the brain. This is commonly called a stroke. Although the cause is less certain, epilepsy is also a brain disorder in which nerve cells in the brain discharge in an abnormal way. This can lead to symptoms ranging from a very brief unnoticeable loss of consciousness, to violent convulsions.

Brain disorders are often divided into two categories. *Acute brain disorders* are temporary disturbances that result from such things as high fever, excessive use of drugs or alcohol, head injury, starvation, tumors or poisoning. The patient is often confused, lethargic, delirious and sometimes unconscious (in a coma) so that he cannot be aroused.

114

If the cause of the disorder is treated, such patients usually can improve and function normally again. *Chronic brain disorders* are more permanent. Often the brain is destroyed or altered in a way which cannot be changed. Treatment can sometimes stop further damage but then the patient must be helped to live within the limitations imposed by his condition.

## PSYCHOSIS

The term *psychosis* refers to abnormal behavior which is so severe that hospitalization is almost always necessary. The patient frequently loses contact with reality and often shows behavior which is unconventional, irrational, confused, unpredictable, and sometimes uncontrollable.

Just as normal people show individual differences in their personality traits and ways of behaving, so there are many different psychotic characteristics. Each patient has his own unique cluster of symptoms, and no two psychotic patients are exactly alike. Even with these differences, however, there are some common characteristics which make it possible to divide the psychoses into three main groupings: schizophrenia, affective disorders, and paranoid states.

### SCHIZOPHRENIA

Roughly half of all patients in mental hospitals are diagnosed as schizophrenics. For most of these patients, the disorder developed slowly and first made its appearance early in life (between childhood and the midforties). According to Eugen Bleuler, the Swiss psychiatrist who first suggested the term *schizophrenia*, there are four basic symptoms.[1] First, there is a *loose thinking*. By this we mean that the patient's thoughts are vague, illogical, rambling, repetitious and meaningless. The following is part of a note which was given to a psychologist just prior to Christmas (the spelling is unchanged):

> How you lick to be Sanata Clause christmas Far Way train winter comeing on beFor we Get Winter Weather could

norther more at christmas time Go true winter the best Fair be New For all christmas christmas Home christmas transportation Find NEW Friend spruce up For christmas the best I now Whe'l way Hour or two or Friend or two For all the Days of christmas chain to snow once again Winter cold for the Winter. . . .

Secondly, the schizophrenic is characterized by *self-centered withdrawal*. He acts in accordance with a fantasy world of his own making. His wishes, fears, beliefs, hallucinations and daydreams are often the only reality he knows. For this reason, communication with the outside world is difficult, and in many cases impossible. Third, there are *disturbances in emotion*. These patients are often depressed, apathetic and aloof. Sometimes they show emotions which are quite inappropriate, such as laughing when they hear sad news. Finally, there may be *ambivalence* in which the schizophrenic vascillates, for example, between sadness and joy, affection and mistrust, or modesty and immodesty.

In addition to these characteristics, schizophrenics often neglect personal hygiene; their posture, gestures and mannerisms can be unusual; they may engage in inappropriate sexual behavior, such as openly masturbating on the ward; they may stop using the toilet and either wet their pants or urinate on the floor; and there can be unusual motor behavior such as pacing up and down, keeping the muscles rigid, imitating the movements of some other person, or engaging in repetitious rituals. In addition to all of this, the schizophrenic sometimes feels that his body and mind are somehow not intact. He may feel that his hands are really plaster, for example, that there are rats eating his brain, or that he is outside of his body looking in.

According to the 1968 diagnostic manual of the American Psychiatric Association, schizophrenic reactions can be divided into several basic categories. These include the following:

*Schizophrenia, simple type.* Here the person shows a grad-

116

ual withdrawal from society. He is often seclusive, apathetic, preoccupied, irresponsible, sloppy, and disinterested in people, but he is still largely in contact with reality. Some of these characteristics are shown in the following interview:

> Doctor: Do you know who I am?
> Patient: A doctor, I suppose.
> Dr.: How do you feel?
> Pt.: Oh—OK, I guess.
> Dr.: Do you know where you are?
> Pt.: It's a hospital.
> Dr.: Why are you here?
> Pt.: I don't know. . . .I don't think I should be here. I'm all right.
> Dr.: Where would you rather be?
> Pt.: I don't care, just out. . .I don't know. Maybe with some fellows or something. I don't care. There were some guys I used to know.
> Dr.: What did you do with those fellows?
> Pt.: I don't know—just go around.
> Dr.: How do you like it here?
> Pt.: I don't know, I don't care. It's all right, I guess. [2]

Since these people do not hallucinate, show delusions, or give evidence of extremely deviant behavior, they often live at home under family care. If the family comes to church, the simple schizophrenic may come along, but he will be a pretty lusterless and inactive member of the congregation.

*Schizophrenia, hebephrenic type.* Shallow emotion, giggling, silly mannerisms, meaningless chatter, and impulsive actions characterize the hebephrenic. One gets the impression that this person has retreated from the stresses of life by regressing to an irresponsible childish level of behavior. Hebephrenic reactions are less common now than they were several years ago, probably because current methods of treatment usually prevent such patients from deteriorating to the extreme forms of silliness.

*Schizophrenia, catatonic type.* These patients alternate between a stupor (in which there is muscular rigidity accompanied by mutism or a stereotyped echoing of the words of others) and frenzied excitement. In some respects, this is like a scared rabbit who freezes in the hopes that he won't be noticed and then runs helter-skelter across a field.

● *Schizophrenia, paranoid type.* Here there is illogical, unrealistic thinking in which the person frequently has a delusion that he is some great person (Christ, for example) or that he is being persecuted. Often there are hallucinations along with attitudes of hostility and aggression. The paranoid's symptoms are frequently related to religious themes, so the person may feel he is a prophet or saint or that he is going to be punished for his sins.

● *Schizophrenia, undifferentiated type.* Many patients do not fit neatly into any of the other schizophrenia categories. These people may show unique symptoms, or a combination of simple, hebephrenic, catatonic, and paranoid symptoms. Such patients usually are diagnosed as *chronic* undifferentiated schizophrenics if the symptoms are gradual and long lasting, or *acute* undifferentiated schizophrenics when the symptoms appear suddenly and disappear after a short period of time.

Currently there is great debate over the causes of schizophrenia. Much of the disagreement centers around the question of whether the disorder is physiologically or psychologically caused. It has been clearly established that schizophrenics, when compared to normals, show biochemical disorders; on the basis of these findings, it has been suggested that the physiological defects *cause* schizophrenia. But it is just as logical to conclude that the biological imbalance is a *result* of schizophrenia. Some have suggested that the schizophrenic's poor home background and life stresses cause the disorder, but it may be that these simply lower resistance so that the person is more susceptible to physiological illness. More research has been devoted to schizophrenia than to any other topic, but the disorder still remains the "most baffling of all psychiatric conditions." [3] As the research continues, it is probably best to conclude that schizophrenia has a number of causes and that the relative importance of these may vary from person to person.

As long as there is great debate over the causes of schizophrenia, there can be "no general agreement as to how schizophrenia should be treated."[4] Many treatment techniques have been tried, but the most common are drugs, milieu therapy, and various types of psychotherapy. Prognosis is best when the disorder has had a sudden onset and a short duration, and when the patient is a young person who has had a history of relatively stable behavior.

## AFFECTIVE DISORDERS

Sometimes called manic-depressive reactions, affective disorders are characterized by intense mood swings, as illustrated in Figure 4-1. In our daily lives, most of us

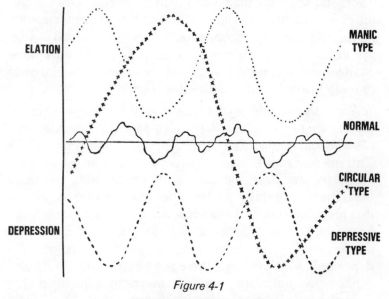

*Figure 4-1*

**Types of Affective Reactions**

The broken lines show the three most common types of affective disorders, the solid line represents the emotional behavior of normal behavior.

vascillate between periods of happiness and discouragement, these feelings depending somewhat on circumstances and somewhat on our personalities. This is illustrated by the solid line. The dotted line represents a manic type of reaction. People with this diagnosis consistently show good humor, excited overactivity, and a great rush of ideas. They are always "high" emotionally, but sometimes this is more so than at other times. The line of dashes illustrates the depressive type of reaction. In contrast to the manic, people in this category are almost always discouraged and dejected. They engage in a minimum of activity and give the impression that life is hopeless and worthless. In circular-type reactions, the patient vascillates between manic and depressive states. This is shown by the line of $x$'s. The circular reactions are least common, comprising about 25 percent of the affective disorders, while the manic and depressive reactions characterize 30 percent and 45 percent of the patients, respectively.[5] Although Figure 4-1 shows smooth curves, the mood swings are likely to be much more irregular. Some patients show changes every few days while others go as long as a year or more before showing noticeable change.

According to one psychologist, "Our exact knowledge of the causes of the manic depressive psychoses is as incomplete as our knowledge of the causes of schizophrenia."[6] Current research evidence suggests that changes in body chemistry may be at the basis of these reactions; but since the frequency of this disorder varies from culture to culture, it is probable that psychological causes are also important. Frequently the disorder arises following a stressful situation and may reflect an "everything will be fine" elation or a depressed "what's the use, there is no hope" attitude. Drugs, shock, psychotherapy, and environmental manipulation have all been effective in treating these patients.

*Involutional reactions* are a special type of affective disorder which usually occur between the ages of forty to fifty-five in women, and fifty to sixty-five in men. People

120

face a number of physical and psychological stresses as they approach the later years in life. Sexual changes, a decrease in energy, declining health, departure of the children from home, uncertainty about the future, disappointment over not having achieved life goals—these and other middle-age problems often cause a person to feel discouraged. While most people rise above these discouragements and meet the challenges of later life, some are unable to do so. They develop the involutional symptoms of depression, sadness, worry, insomnia, restlessness, excessive concern about health, and (often) paranoid ideas. The disorder often disappears spontaneously after two or three years, but recovery can usually be speeded up by shock treatment accompanied by psychotherapy.

## PARANOID STATES.

Unlike the paranoid schizophrenic, people who are given this diagnosis are quite capable of getting along in society. Their behavior often appears to be normal except for the fact that they have well-thought-out delusional beliefs which are usually based on one false premise. Once the basic premise is accepted, the delusional system often appears to be very logical. Once a woman decides that her husband is unfaithful, for example, or once a pastor concludes that he is not liked by the congregation, it is easy to misinterpret and twist the meaning of other people's behavior in order to find evidence which supports the delusion. One lady, whom the author knew, concluded that people were watching her and that every car which passed her home contained spies. It is not difficult to imagine how this lady would have reacted if, for example, she saw a young couple drive by who happened to admire the roses in her yard.

Sometimes when two or more people live together for a while they share a delusion and convince each other of its truth. Thus whole groups and sometimes whole churches have become paranoid. Once it is assumed that all teenagers are bad, that Billy Graham is a heretic, or that the country

121

is infiltrated by Communist spies, it is easy to find evidence (however flimsy) that can be interpreted as supporting the premise. Contradictory evidence, of course, is ignored.

Most paranoids live in the community, believe their delusions, but don't really bother anyone. Sometimes, however, these people can be very dangerous, especially if they decide to take matters into their own hands and "deal with" their enemies directly.

It is generally believed that the paranoid develops his delusions in order to hide socially unacceptable impulses from himself, and to project his feelings onto someone else. A delusion that "someone is trying to seduce me" is safer than acknowledging one's own sexual urges. "Men like me" is less threatening than "I'm a homosexual who is attracted to other men." "My congregation dislikes me" is more socially acceptable than "I hate the people in my church."

Treatment of the paranoid disorders is long and very difficult because the delusional system is highly developed, is "supported by (assumed) evidence," and is necessary for the paranoid to keep if he is to hide his impulses from himself and from others. Often the counselor's intentions are misinterpreted and even incorporated into the delusional beliefs (e.g., "he's just a spy like the rest," or "he's trying to hurt me also").

## NEUROSIS

All of us need love, emotional security, feelings of self-esteem, and freedom from excessive anxiety or guilt. "A neurosis, or psychoneurosis—the terms mean the same thing—is a disorder in which these needs are not gratified sufficiently."[7] The neurotic feels anxious, unhappy, insecure, guilty or unloved, but he struggles to keep these feelings in check by clinging to a number of defensive techniques. He does not show extreme signs of abnormality. There are no hallucinations or delusions; he is well-oriented, his thinking is rational, and he rarely requires hospitalization. Table 4-1 compares the neurotic's behavior with that of the psychotic.

## Comparison of Neurosis and Psychosis

| Neurosis | Psychosis |
|---|---|
| Can distinguish between reality and fantasy. | Cannot distinguish between reality and fantasy. |
| Oriented to the environment (knows who he is, the date, where he is, accurate details of his environment, etc.). | Disoriented. |
| Shows anxiety and physical symptoms but no hallucinations, delusions, or extremely unusual behavior. | Often shows hallucinations, delusions, strange behavior. |
| Often has some insight into the nature of his behavior. Frequently motivated to change. | Rarely has insight into his behavior. Often not motivated to change. |
| Is socially sensitive. Conforms, in general, to the expectations of society. Rarely injures himself or others. | Not sensitive to others. Ignores social expectations. Often a danger to himself and to others. |
| Can manage his own affairs. Rarely requires hospitalization. | Cannot manage his affairs. Hospitalization is usually necessary. |

Table 4-1

123

It has been estimated that, in the United States alone, there are at least 10 or 11 million neurotics—roughly 5 percent of the population.[8] These people come from all walks of life, all age groups, and all socioeconomic classes. They include the well-educated and the poorly educated, the successful and the unsuccessful, active church members and those who are not interested in religion.

GENERAL CHARACTERISTICS OF NEUROSIS

Like all people with problems, neurotics differ from one another in the behavior which they typically show, but a few characteristics seem to be especially prevalent. The pastor or other counselor should be alert to these.

*Anxiety.* This is an emotional response of dread and apprehension. Sometimes, as with an actor who is anxious about a coming performance, the person can identify the source of his anxiety. More often, the individual feels threatened and uncomfortable but is unable to pinpoint the cause of this feeling.

Anxiety is the most common characteristic of neurosis. Sometimes the anxiety is mild, but more frequently it is intense and incapacitating. Usually an individual can cover up his anxiety, but sometimes it slips out in the form of physical symptoms or unusual behavior. While the anxiety may flare up at times into acutely felt *anxiety attacks*, it is usually experienced as a vague feeling of insecurity.

*Tension and hypersensitivity.* All of us have observed runners waiting at the starting line for the gun sound that will begin the race. These athletes are tense. Their bodies are mobilized, ready to go as soon as they get the signal. Not infrequently, these races get off to a false start because runners "jump the gun" and start the race before the pistol fires. Apparently the athletes are so mobilized for action that they react to even mild sounds.

For runners, the tension and increased sensitivity usually are of a relatively short duration. The neurotic, however, is continually mobilized for action and likely to jump at

124

even the slightest provocation. He is easily irritated, unable to take criticism, and prone to "blow up" and overreact in response to even minor issues.

*Physical complaints and symptoms.* It should come as no surprise that the person who is anxious and tense is also likely to develop physical ailments. As we will see later, emotional reactions are always accompanied by changes in physical functioning. If a state of tension or an emotionlike anxiety exists for several days or months, for example, eventually there will be some breakdown in body functioning, with accompanying symptoms. Sometimes neurotics also experience physical symptoms for which there is no corresponding organic disease. They may have trouble seeing, back pain, prolonged fatigue, stiffness of the arms and legs, or other symptoms, even though physicians can find nothing organically wrong.

*Trouble getting along with people.* With his anxieties, tensions and physical concerns, the neurotic is very much aware of himself. This causes him to be selfish, demanding and frequently insensitive to the needs of other people. When others don't bow to his demands, he is likely to sulk, become hostile, or engage in other childish behavior.

*Rigidity.* The neurotic develops specific defenses in an attempt to reduce his feelings of anxiety and insecurity. When new situations come along, he falls back on these old ways of reacting and behaves in a rigid stereotyped fashion. Apparently he is unable to appraise a new situation and change his behavior accordingly.

*Unhappiness.* Obviously a person who experiences so many difficulties cannot be very happy. The neurotic feels inadequate to face the pressures of life but he does not know how to overcome his inadequacies. As a result he feels discouraged, pessimistic, and generally dissatisfied with life. According to Coleman, the neurotic is "like a motorist on a mountain road who is terrified by signs warning of dangerous curves. By shutting his eyes to such warnings,

125

he protects himself from anxiety but at the expense of lowering his driving efficiency and making himself more liable to accidents."[9]

Very often these people find their way into churches where they hope to find relief from their anxiety and tension.* Sometimes the pastor, a deacon, or some other church member becomes a sympathetic listener as the neurotic talks about his ailments and troubles. But these people often make themselves unpopular because they can be very demanding and have no apparent awareness that the listener may have other important things to do with his time.

## TYPES OF NEUROSIS

Sometimes neurotics exhibit one or two dominant symptoms. Based on these characteristic signs, psychiatrists and psychologists have divided the neuroses into several subtypes. These include the following:

*Anxiety neurosis.* The major characteristics of the anxiety neuroses are tension, prolonged apprehension, and a preoccupation about possible calamities. This unsettled state persists no matter how well things seem to be going, and is periodically interrupted by *anxiety attacks* in which the individual is suddenly overwhelmed by terror and intense panic.

> David, a 28-year-old man who was serving a prison sentence for robbery, referred himself to the prison psychologist for a few weeks before he was due to be released. He complained that for several weeks he had been finding it difficult to sleep and that during the day he was bothered by unexplainable panic and tension. At night, when alone in his cell, he complained that he could hear his heart beating loudly and irregularly, that he felt suffocated and that he found it difficult to breathe. These feelings and symptoms had become gradually worse until they reached a point where he sought help at the prison hospital.

*One writer has written an entire book dealing with neurotics in the church (R.J.St.Clair, *Neurotics in the Church*).

126

Quite apart from the unpleasantness of his condition, David was especially upset by his inability to think of anything which had happened recently to account for these fears. On the contrary, he pointed out that he was expecting to be released soon—a release to which he had been looking forward with enthusiasm. His wife was waiting for him and his employer had agreed to find him a job.

As David and the psychologist talked, it became apparent that anxiety like this had occurred once before. It had happened when David was serving with the Army during the early months of the Vietnamese war. The symptoms which he described were much the same and had developed several weeks before he was due to be returned home and released from military service. During combat duty he had had no problems of this kind, and he had attributed his symptoms to a lack of sleep and the excessive heat.

Prolonged counseling with David revealed that his marriage contained many things which were threatening to him. In fact, the circumstances of the crime for which he was imprisoned were such that it seemed probable that he committed it in order to be arrested—perhaps thus being able to escape from his unbearable home situation. The coming release from prison, like the previous anticipation of release from the Army, served to bring David close to the dreaded home situation. As he got closer to his return home David got more and more anxious and had periodic anxiety attacks. [10]

These anxiety attacks occur most frequently when the individual is faced with threatening situations, such as the need to make an important decision, guilt over some past behavior, a threat to one's status, or fears that some undesirable impulse will become obvious to other people, or—as in David's case—an unconscious unwillingness to return to a tense home setting.

Of course, neurotic people differ in the severity of their anxiety reactions. In the more extreme forms, the individual may experience sleeplessness, outbursts of aggression, attacks of weeping, intense feelings of inadequacy, and frequent anxiety attacks. In the milder anxiety neuroses, a person may simply appear timid, tense, easily embarrassed and prone to worry. Such people are overly conscientious and have difficulty making decisions because they are afraid of making mistakes. Frequently the anxiety leads to physical illnesses and complaints.

It will be recognized that there are many anxious and insecure people in our churches. Usually we describe them as being "high strung" or "nervous." Since they tend to get flustered easily and find it hard to make decisions, they usually get along best when they are not in leadership positions.

"Taking the pressure off" is one way of helping these people. It is also good if they can discover that others remain calm in stressful situations. In addition we should remember that several Bible passages have comforting words for times of anxiety. For example, Matthew 11:28-30; John 14:1-3, 27; and Philippians 4:6-7 can be helpful to all believers in times of difficulty. With an anxious person it is also helpful to get at the source of anxiety if this can be done. Sometimes a pastor or Christian friend can talk with the person about the things which make him anxious; but when the anxiety is persistent and intense, the help of a skilled pastoral counselor or trained therapist should be sought.

Before leaving this topic we should emphasize that not all anxiety is bad. As we noted in an earlier chapter, anxiety is often what motivates young people to study for exams. Likewise, anxiety over a sermon or speech often leads to more diligent preparation and a greater dependence on the guidance of the Holy Spirit. Clearly, then, mild anxiety motivates, but intense anxiety incapacitates. At times we all experience both mild and intense anxiety; but for the neurotic, anxiety is ever present and often incapacitating.

*Hysterical neurosis.* This has nothing to do with a person becoming hysterical. It is, instead, a type of neurosis in which the individual's anxiety causes him to have physical

128

pains or complaints, even though there is nothing organically wrong. He may, for example, experience blindness, deafness, paralysis, backaches, inability to talk, constipation, diarrhea, stomach upsets, or loss of appetite, but physicians can find nothing to cause these symptoms. Even though there is nothing organically wrong, the symptoms are nevertheless very real. The person with neurotic blindness, for example, really can't see, and the person with a conversion backache will really experience intense pain.

These persons often show an unusually blasé attitude and lack of concern about their symptoms, but the physical ailments serve a real purpose, nevertheless. They may prevent the patient from facing unpleasant situations, for example, and in addition bring forth a lot of sympathy from one's friends. The man who has a bad back and can't work, gets workman's compensation and avoids the threat of being fired. The student who develops paralysis of the arm can't write, but he also can't fail his courses if this "ailment" makes it necessary for him to drop out of school. The lady who loses her sense of smell can't tell when her teenage son has been drinking, and this prevents a lot of anxiety.

In treating this disorder, removal of symptoms by hypnosis or suggestion can be effective, but the best treatment is to help the person to directly face the conflict or stress that is causing the neurosis. If the source of anxiety can be removed, there is no longer any need to hide behind the protection of a physical symptom. Of course it can be embarrassing to have a complaint clear up suddenly, so hysterical neurotics often cling to their symptoms, even after the original source of anxiety is gone.

Writers of abnormal psychology textbooks have frequently pointed out that hysterical symptoms are often removed quickly by faith healers and miracle cures. These techniques are thought to be especially effective with the neurotic because such people are highly suggestible and like to be the center of attention. As a result, they are easily influenced by the words of the faith healer or the exciting ceremonial and religious services at a shrine. Their desire for attention is met as people pray for them and express concern over the illness. The "healing" often takes place in front of a crowd of people who subsequently shower much attention on the "healed" individual. Of course, it should not be assumed that people who seek such cures are insincere or consciously seeking attention. Most are in dead earnest and come in a "psychological state of expectant excitement." [11] If they are converted to a new religious belief at the time of their healing, the original anxieties often disappear, there is no longer a need for the old symptoms, and the "cure" is permanent. If there is simply a removal of a symptom and no change in one's life situation, the same old anxieties will persist and before long either the old symptom may return or a new one may appear in its place.

Most Christian psychologists would probably agree that a large number of the "cures" seen in healing meetings or at shrines like Lourdes can be explained as the removal of hysterical symptoms. This explanation for some faith healing cannot hide the fact, however, that supernatural divine healing still occurs. Scripture teaches this (Ja. 5:13-15), and even in the writings of psychologists who do not identify themselves as Christians, there is a recognition that unexplainable cures occur in people who in no way show symptoms of hysterical neurosis. "The world is full of phenomena that cannot be explained by the conceptual schemes current at a particular time," wrote one respected psychologist. "Today these include inexplicable cures of fatal illnesses, in secular as well as religious settings. Depending on one's theoretical predilections, one may choose to believe that all, none, or some of these are miraculous." [12] The author of this book is inclined to choose the latter alternative. Psychologists can explain some of what is called divine healing, but they cannot account for all of it. God still answers the petitions of His people as they pray for the sick.

Before we leave this brief discussion of faith healing, two concluding comments should be made. First, we should remember that just because man can explain something it does not follow that God has therefore withdrawn. We may be able to "explain" faith healing (as we can explain the stages of plant growth or the movement of the stars in their orbits), but this does not make the explained event any less wonderful or mean that it is not divinely created. God works in ways that we understand as well as in ways that are beyond our comprehension. Second, we must realize that God does not heal all of those who ask for healing. Paul's "thorn in the flesh" apparently was never taken away. Instead, its continued presence helped a Christian to grow in the faith (2 Co. 1:8-9; 12:7-10).

*Phobic neurosis.* Almost everybody has heard of "claustrophobia," the fear of closed spaces. For reasons which they can't understand, some people are acutely uncomfortable if they have to enter an elevator, a small hallway, or any other narrow space. The person who experiences these feelings may recognize that his behavior is foolish and may even laugh at himself, but he still feels anxious about enclosed spaces and may go far out of his way to avoid the thing which he fears. People with claustrophobia sometimes climb several flights of stairs rather than enter the enclosed space of an elevator, and they have been known to sit up all night in a train in order to avoid the pullman compartment.

A phobic reaction can be defined as an overwhelming and persistent fear of some harmless object or situation. While claustrophobia is probably the best known, people fear a great number of things, including high places (acrophobia), open spaces (agoraphobia), thunder and lightning (astraphobia), blood (hematophobia), crowds (ochlophobia), water (hydrophobia), germs (mysophobia), darkness (nysto-

131

phobia), fire (pyrophobia), or animals (zoophobia). Since we can develop irrational fears over anything, it is correct to say that there can be as many phobias as there are objects and situations.

Why do phobias develop? There appear to be at least three common causes. First, some people have learned their fears. The author knows a lady who has a phobia about the color green. She refuses to wear green, decorate her home in green, or keep plants in the house. This is an irrational fear which she jokingly attributes to superstition, but the phobia began when her child was killed in an automobile accident. At that time the child was wearing green clothing, and the grieving mother came to associate green with death. This one learning experience was the basis for a lifelong phobia.

For a second group of people, phobias may be a defense against some dangerous impulse. If a housewife is consciously or unconsciously afraid of stabbing someone, a fear of knives will keep her away from these implements and will help keep the aggressive impulses in check. If this seems to be an extreme example, the reader might think of someone who has a fear of height. Often such people will openly admit that they are "afraid I might jump." To protect themselves against such impulses, they develop an intense fear of high places.

Finally, phobias sometimes develop to divert attention from more threatening situations. One man, for example, opened a small business which, after a few months, began to fail. At about the same time, the man began to notice that his shop was stuffy and small. His discomfort in the small shop became a convenient excuse for closing and diverted attention from the fact that he was a business failure.

Phobias can be treated in a variety of ways. Occasionally it is helpful to discuss this. An individual can, by himself, learn to slowly accept the feared object without feeling fearful, but in most cases professional help is advisable. Often within a very few sessions a skilled counselor can help to eliminate or at least reduce the strength of a phobia.

*Obsessive-compulsive neurosis.* As children, most of us played the little game where we avoided stepping on sidewalk cracks, lest this "break your mother's back" or bring some other dire consequence. These childish rituals are common, harmless and usually temporary. It is only when behavior such as this persists, or gets its start in adulthood, that we describe it as a compulsion, an irresistible urge to engage in some senseless or meaningless activity. While a compulsion is an urge to *act*, an obsession refers to the persistent recurrence of some unpleasant impulse or *thought*. These compulsive actions and obsessive thoughts usually occur together in the same individual, although one frequently dominates. Obsessions and compulsions are often intense and likely to interfere with daily behavior. In every case they persist because they protect the individual from anxiety that might otherwise be overwhelming.

> George is a college freshman who came to the counseling center because he was having difficulties adjusting to campus life. Whenever he had an appointment, George arrived promptly on time. When he entered the office he took off his watch, placed it on the desk where he could see it, indicated what he wanted to discuss, and stated the number of minutes to be spent on each topic. He often asked specific questions, took detailed notes, and left promptly after 50 minutes.

As long as one's world is this organized, one can feel secure and able to predict the future. Let this order be disrupted and the individual becomes highly anxious, insecure, and possibly immobilized.

Around the turn of the century, Sigmund Freud wrote a paper in which he suggested that religion is a "universal obsessional neurosis." All religious ceremonial, he concluded, is compulsive activity which keeps us from becoming anxious over our impulses, "our sense of guilt," or our fear of divine vengeance. By implication, all church members were considered to be obsessive-compulsive neurotics.

Few readers of this book are likely to agree completely with Freud's analysis, but we must recognize, nevertheless, that there is often a lot of obsessive and compulsive behavior within the church. Repetitious reciting of creeds, persistent repeating of stereotyped prayers, and other kinds of rituals often help to alleviate and avoid anxiety concerning past sin. In less formal churches, people sometimes become compulsive over such matters as personal devotions or church attendance. If they do not pray and read their Bibles every day without fail, or if they miss the midweek prayer meeting, these people feel intensely anxious. In themselves, all of these religious practices are desirable, and for many they provide meaningful worship experiences. For the compulsive these rituals are much less meaningful, but missing them brings feelings of guilt and distress. When our lives have degenerated into such legalistic drugery, we have lost the joy of Christian living and have become slaves to religious compulsiveness. Our lives have become unfruitful and boring rather than full and "abundant" (Jn. 10:10). By confessing sin and inviting the Holy Spirit to take control, Christian service and fellowship with God can become a joy (1 Jn. 1:9; Gal. 5:22).

In treating obsessive-compulsive reactions, professional counselors usually attempt to find why people become slaves to these repetitious thoughts and actions. If treatment comes early, the source of anxiety and the resulting symptoms often disappear. When the obsessive-compulsive reaction is well established, therapeutic treatment often takes longer and sometimes isn't very successful.

*Depressive neurosis.* At times, all of us become discouraged and saddened by the circumstances of life. When a loved one dies, when we fail in some venture, or when we experience financial setbacks, it is natural that we should be discouraged—at least for a while.

In the neurotic depressive reactions, discouragement is exceptionally intense and lasts for a long period of time. The depressed person appears dejected and sad. His posture droops, and he sometimes has bags under his eyes. Often there are a high level of anxiety, lowered self-confidence, a slowing down of his movements, difficulty in concentrating, sleep disturbances, a loss of interest in other people and things, a lower level of activity, a feeling of hopelessness, and vaguely felt hostility.

In almost all cases, the depression is in response to some environmental stress with which the individual cannot cope. Often the interest and support of a sympathetic pastor, counselor or friend can assist such people during their long period of discouragement, especially if this emotional support can be supplemented with antidepressant drugs, electroshock therapy, or brief hospitalization. But such treatment is not always appreciated by the depressed. They may show hostility toward the counselor, sulk, and refuse to be swayed by sympathy. Many times they try to manipulate others, but they have an aversion to being manipulated. [13]

Sometimes the depressed person finds life so discouraging that the only way out seems to be suicide (see Table 4-2), occasionally preceded by the murder of loved ones. Usually people who are contemplating suicide give prior warning of their intentions (see Table 4-3). These warning signals are really a "cry for help" which the alert pastor or another concerned person can recognize. [14] When such signs are observed, it is well to be supportive and to refer the individual for professional help. Several cities now have suicide-prevention centers which people can call if they are contemplating self-destruction. The number is listed in the telephone book under "suicide."

# Table 4-2
## FACTS ABOUT SUICIDE*

**Incidence**

General

200,000 attempts in the U. S. each year; over 25,000 successful. Suicide ranks 9th as cause of death in the U.S. Largest number occur in spring, during morning, Monday or Tuesday. Most common methods: firearms, jumping from high places, sleeping pills, gas, poison, and hanging.

Age and sex

Three times as many men as women kill themselves, but women more often make halfhearted, unsuccessful attempts. Over half of persons who kill themselves are over 45. Divorced have highest rate, widowed and single next; 22 percent live alone.

Occupation

All occupations represented; incidence highest among professional groups, especially lawyers, dentists and physicians; low among ministers.

Sociocultural

More common among urban than rural people. Low in Japan and certain strong Catholic countries like Ireland; high in some Iron Curtain countries. Less common during crises like war and earthquakes; more common during depressions.

**Causes**

Physical illness

About 40 percent of men and 20 percent of women kill themselves because of ill health.

Mental illness

About 35 percent kill themselves while temporarily disturbed emotionally, usually during a period of severe depression.

Guilt and hostility

Severe guilt feelings or intense hostility may be turned inward against self, making injury to self the only apparent solution to problems.

Losses

Individual may commit suicide after death of loved one he feels he cannot live without (usually mate after long, happy marriage) or after financial reverses, injuries, or other losses which require too great a change in way of life or intolerable lowering of status or self-evaluation.

Revenge

Suicide occasionally based on spite—to make others feel guilty; sometimes person only intends to scare others but succeeds by accident, as when overcome by gas fumes.

*Adapted from J. C. Coleman and W. Broen, *Abnormal Psychology and Modern Life*, p. 339.

136

## Table 4-3

### INDICATORS OF INTENTION TO ATTEMPT SUICIDE:
### A CHECKLIST*

1. History of previous attempts (persons who tried before will often try again)............................. _____

2. Talk of suicide (It is not true that people who talk about suicide won't try it. Most people talk about it before the attempt.)........................ _____

3. Ideas of guilt and worthlessness............................ _____

4. Feelings of hopelessness.................................... _____

5. Environmental setbacks (like divorce, financial loss, death in the family, etc)......................... _____

6. Preoccupation with insomnia.............................. _____

7. Excessive concern about physical pains and illnesses.............. _____

8. Sudden and unexplainable shift to a happy, cheerful mood.......... _____

9. Looking after one's affairs (like making sure one has a will, paying one's bills, etc.)......................... _____

10. Knowledge regarding the best methods of suicide (Shooting, drugs, and carbon monoxide work best. Wrist-slashing is rarely successful)......................................... _____

*Adapted from E. S. Shneidman, N. L. Farberow and R. E. Litman, *The Psychology of Suicide.*

*Neurasthenic neurosis.* Some people seem to be always tired and lacking in energy. They complain of overwork, have various aches and pains, are often irritable, do not express much interest in life, and rarely feel up to doing much of anything.

This perpetual feeling of exhaustion and weakness is the chief characteristic of neurasthenic neurosis. Most often this is seen in people whose lives are characterized by frustration and boredom. Housewives, for example, who feel neglected by their husbands and left to the seemingly endless chores of cleaning house and looking after children, often complain of perpetual fatigue. The symptoms may persist even after a considerable rest; but if the "victim" is given the opportunity to engage in some activity that he or she likes, a burst of enthusiastic energy may suddenly appear.

Like all neurotic behavior, neurasthenic reactions help people to cope with and sometimes to avoid the pressures of life. If he is "always exhausted," a person can expect sympathy from others and he has an excuse for not completing daily routine chores.

As we have already implied, physical rest or the use of drugs is not very effective in helping neurasthenic people. More valuable are attempts to change the individual's life situation and to help him or her find some new purpose in living. Obviously such treatment must be highly individualistic since that which gives meaning to the life of one person may have little influence on the life of another. Perhaps the church can have an important ministry in meeting the needs of these people.

*Other neuroses.* A number of other neurotic reactions have been observed and discussed in the psychological literature. *Hypochondriacal neurosis*, for example, describes the people who develop a morbid concern about their health. Such people, to whom we usually refer as hypochondriacs, often avoid the responsibilities and pressures of life by their excessive concern about body functioning. *Mixed neurosis*

138

is a diagnosis given to those people who have a combination of the above symptoms.

## THE CAUSES AND TREATMENT OF NEUROSIS

By developing neurotic symptoms, many people are enabled to get along even when they are faced with highly stressful situations. The symptoms of neurosis invariably serve some useful purpose, although the neurotic is not consciously aware of this. The purposes include removing oneself from an unpleasant situation; gaining status, attention or affection from others; punishing oneself in order to alleviate guilt; punishing others; and receiving monetary compensation from insurance companies. (Kutash, 1965).

Neurotic symptoms do nothing to really solve a problem, but they do hide problems and shield the person from anxiety. Thus, while drugs and other medical procedures may alleviate the symptoms, lasting improvement only comes as the individual faces and copes with his stress. This is probably done best with the help of a professional counselor, but many neurotics also show significant improvement as a result of talking with a sympathetic friend. Because of this, pastors, Sunday school teachers, and other concerned individuals can frequently help the neurotic individual to cope more effectively with stress when it comes along. Christian counselors should not overlook the value of spiritual practices such as Scripture reading and prayer. These are useful auxiliaries to the "works" of concern, listening, and helping people reach practical solutions to their problems.

## PERSONALITY DISORDERS

The personality disorders (sometimes called character disorders) are deeply ingrained ways of behaving that develop early in life and make it difficult for the person to get along efficiently. This is not something that only appears in times of great stress. It is maladjusted behavior which develops over the years and becomes characteristic of the individual's way of life. Most people in this group

139

are not aware that their behavior is deviant. They feel no anxiety or distress, and if they come for counseling it is usually because they have been persuaded to do so by their families or the courts. The major characteristic of these people is not an internal anxiety or feeling of turmoil. Instead, they act in ways which are often considered to be odd or antisocial. Some of the most common ways of responding are discussed below. The church leader will recognize that people such as these can be found in almost every congregation.

*Paranoid personality.* This type of person is very sensitive about his relationships with other people. He is always suspicious and ever alert to the possibility that someone might wish to harm or outsmart him. Because of these suspicions, the paranoid is often cantankerous, critical, and intent on "getting even." He is envious, jealous, rigid and stubborn. As a result, he is not popular and often has very few friends.

Paranoid personalities are sometimes found in the church. They are the members who conclude that people are talking about them, that they are not appreciated, or that the pastor is "out to make life difficult" for them. Sometimes they react with hostility, sarcasm and stubbornness, and periodically they move—in a huff—from church to church.

It is regretful that these traits are also seen at times in whole congregations. For the most part, such groups sincerely desire to remain "true to the faith"; but in their attempts to do this, they become suspicious of everyone who is not a member of their group. Other individuals and congregations, even within the same denomination, are verbally attacked on the slightest provocation. There is a refusal to cooperate with other evangelical missionary societies or with organizations such as Inter-Varsity Christian Fellowship or the Billy Graham Association. In addition to their suspicions and critical attitudes, the paranoid congregations often show the other paranoid characteristics: jealousy, rigidity, stubbornness and hostility. Every so often these congregations break off from their denominations to form splinter groups of their own.

At times, we all blame others for the shortcomings which we are reluctant to face within ourselves. But paranoid personalities (and perhaps paranoid congregations) do this to an excessive degree, and often they misinterpret the behavior of others. Sometimes paranoids provoke others to act in hostile or other undesirable ways. Then the undesirable behavior is held up as proof of one's suspicions. Individual A, for example, may strongly and unfairly criticize individual B. When B responds with anger, A can say, "See? That proves what kind of a person he is!" Of course it is difficult to reason with such people because of their stubbornness and suspicion. For this reason, therapy is not very successful. Instead, the church leader must learn to respond patiently and with kindness, trusting that the love of God will bring a change of heart.

*Cyclothymic personality*. This term describes people who are highly extroverted, gregarious and friendly. Often such persons appear to have boundless energy and enthusiasm. They are frequently successful in their work, competent in social situations, and actively involved in many community projects. Those who are church members are often very active. At times, however, these people also have mood swings in which they plunge into pessimistic despair. Often these changes of mood come without warning and have nothing to do with changes in the environment.

It is difficult to determine the causes of cyclothymic behavior, or to give concise guidelines for treatment. As with all of the personality disorders, the causes and successful treatment depend somewhat on the individual. Since this type of person gets along fine in society, it is probably best to leave him alone unless he gets overly enthusiastic. At such times his enthusiasm may be tempered somewhat by confronting him with more realistic alternatives.

*Schizoid personality*. Shyness and aloofness are the most

141

outstanding characteristics of people in this category. There is a tendency to avoid social contacts and an inability to develop warm relationships with others. Because of their seclusion, schizoid people are sometimes thought of as being odd, eccentric or "in another world."

The roots of this behavior can usually be traced back to childhood experiences. Children who persistently fail or those who come from unstable homes may want to remove themselves from a threatening world. As they grow older, therefore, these children show an increasing tendency to withdraw into themselves, so that it becomes more and more difficult for them to distinguish what is real from what is imagination. They become shy, retiring "loners" who engage in an unusual amount of fantasy, but in spite of this, they often are able to make some adjustments throughout life. Others, however, withdraw so far into their own little worlds that hospitalization becomes necessary.

Since lifelong habits are not easily changed, the treatment of schizoid personality disorders is not very successful. The most realistic approach seems to be one of recognizing the schizoid's limitations and helping him to function as effectively as possible within these limits.

*Obsessive-compulsive personality.* Rigid, meticulous, overconscientious people fit into this category. Such individuals cannot relax and often work incessantly, placing high, perfectionistic, somewhat unattainable demands upon themselves.

One compulsive person described her behavior as follows:

> I am incessantly concerned over the fact that I am not going to get done all I want to. I always have several lists, some very extensive, and as I do the task I cross it out. I try to make a concise list of what I plan or want for the week. During the week I will add to it, but I never cross something off as being unnecessary. Even on my day off, I get up early to do something on my list. I only wish there were more than twenty-four hours in a day.[15]

This behavior is often seen in college students, pastors and other professional people. In order to meet the demands of certain academic programs (like a PhD program or a very demanding seminary curriculum), it is often necessary for students to become rigid, highly organized and perfectionistic. Once these habits have been built up, they sometimes carry over into later life. If the individual is employed in a work situation which is highly demanding, the compulsive personality pattern may persist because "this is the only way to get things done." When the compulsive person tries to become less rigid and demanding, he often experiences guilt and anxiety.

It may be that pride plays a part in this behavior pattern. The compulsive person somehow gets the idea that the world revolves around him. Sometimes it is well to remind such people about President Kennedy's assasination. Here the most important man in the world was suddenly removed from the scene, but life went on. Even our own private lives are likely to continue if we don't finish everything on our list of projects. In our highly aggressive North American culture, perhaps all of us must learn to periodically slow down and "be still." Otherwise the years ahead will show an increase instead of a decrease in compulsive, frenzied behavior.

*Passive-aggressive personality*. Three main types of passive-aggresive reactions have been identified. Often an individual is characterized by just one of these types, but for some people all three are present at times. The *passive-dependent* types are helpless, indecisive and clinging. They need and demand strong emotional support, especially in times of stress. *Passive-aggressive* behavior is seen in people who are stubborn, negativistic, pouting, sulking procrastinators. These people have no need to cling, but they are nevertheless unable to stand on their own two feet. They get in the way of others and, although they are hostile, they rarely show active aggression. The *aggressive* types show outbursts of irritability, tantrums, fighting, and destructive behavior. Kisker suggests that these people have a "nobody's-going-to-push-me-around" attitude. They "carry the proverbial chips on their shoulder. . .[ and] take every frustration in life as a personal affront."[16]

Certainly such people have not learned how to handle their frustrations. When stress comes along, the passive-dependent person clings, the aggressive person is hostile, and the passive-aggressive individual is somewhere in between. Some authors believe that in all three categories, the individual is overly dependent on others and resents this dependency.

Deep, intensive psychotherapy would probably help such people. More often, however, treatment consists of learning more appropriate ways to handle frustration.

*Inadequate personality.* At times, all of us have encountered people who seem to be fumbling through life and living behind a long string of failures. Such people live in society but cannot cope effectively with society's demands. They show poor judgment, an inability to plan or persevere, a lack of foresight, a difficulty in adjusting to new situations, a low energy level, and an inability to handle money wisely. They tend to sink to the lower end of the socioeconomic scale and often must live on welfare payments. In social situations they say the wrong things, act inappropriately, and seem oblivious to hints and other subtle forms of social communications. Sometimes these people cling to the pastor and expect constant encouragement and help in making even minor decisions.

> Ray, a single twenty-four-year old male, periodically attended the college-age class of a large Methodist church. He came for counseling at the urging of another member of the class who had tried to befriend Ray because he seemed such a "loner."
>
> Ray had always been shy and unable to take responsibility.

Although his intelligence was above average, as established by psychological testing, he had gone through high school with a poor academic record and had never attended college. He had held a number of different jobs, but had either quit or been fired from each of them. When he came for counseling, he was employed as a janitor's helper in an office building, but he was thinking of quitting since he didn't like the job.

Loneliness was one of Ray's problems. He had never had a date and was so lacking in self-confidence that he just assumed that no one would ever want to go out with him. He had always been a poor athlete, had never had any real friends, and was uncertain how he should act when around other people. On two occasions he had met strangers who had befriended him and then stolen his money and taken advantage of him sexually. Drifting into the church, he had hoped to find someone who would accept him but he was largely unnoticed because of his shyness and decision not to participate in the activities of his Sunday School class.

Ray was the youngest in a family which included two older sisters. The father was a farmer who had little self-confidence, few friends, and no desire to participate in church or community activities. The mother was a little more outgoing, but her interests were centered in her home and in her desire to train the daughters to be good housekeepers. Ray was largely ignored and, as far back as he can remember, the family assumed that he would "never amount to much."

Ray's life has been characterized by consistent failure. He came for counseling reluctantly and wasn't very motivated to work on his problems since he assumed that life for him could never be different.

It is not known for certain why some people are so inefficient and unable to adequately handle themselves. Apparently many have never learned how to act appropriately. Often this is because they have never had a parent or other adult to serve as a model of efficient, mature and socially adequate behavior. Occasionally inadequate people come from wealthy families where everything has been provided. As children they learn to be overly dependent and then they stay this way on into adulthood.

Therapeutic treatment with these people is not very successful. Their inadequate behavior is deeply ingrained, and they have little desire to change. Perhaps the best that a church leader can do is to help them with their specific problems, serve as a model of successful adult behavior, and try to teach them how to react in specific social, economic, occupational, religious or other situations. If their demands are excessive, one can graciously but firmly place limits on the times and frequency of phone calls.

*Immature personality.* Sometimes people regress to childish behavior in order to get what they want. We are all familiar with the adult who throws temper tantrums, the woman who runs home to mother after family disagreements, or the middle-aged man who chases young girls and avoids family responsibilities by partying with the boys.

These immature people tend to be impulsive, moody, and largely unable to control their emotions. They react to stress by reverting to some behavior which was successful in solving problems during childhood. If in the past this immature behavior "worked" to get the person what he wanted, it is unlikely that there will be any inclination to change later in life. For this reason, therapy is not very helpful.

In dealing with this kind of person, the church leader or the family might try at least two techniques. They can refuse to give in when the immature person shows childish behavior, or they can reward him (by giving what he wants) whenever he shows more mature forms of behavior. In order to work, such techniques would have to be used for long periods of time and must be applied consistently. This takes infinite patience and is likely to be met at first by an increase, rather than a decrease, of immature behavior.

*Emotionally unstable personality.* In the face of minor stress, some people "fall apart" emotionally. Unable to keep control of their feelings, these individuals show great excitement, intense sobbing, or uncontrollable panic.

Studies have shown that emotionally unstable individuals are often unconsciously hostile, guilty and anxious. In order to keep these impulses hidden, such people quickly react to stress with emotional outbursts. If this analysis is correct, therapy should consist first of reducing the hostility, guilt and anxiety, and then teaching more appropriate ways of handling stress. But these goals are very difficult to achieve. Hostility, for example, is usually deep-seated, unconscious, and hard to eliminate. Teaching people to act maturely is not something which occurs overnight. For most unstable people, therefore, it seems best to protect them from stress when possible, and to give encouragement and support when upsetting experiences do come along.

## PSYCHOPHYSIOLOGICAL DISORDERS

Whenever we are afraid or anxious, we often notice a number of physical changes. Our heart may beat faster, breathing may become irregular, the throat may become dry, and we may feel a tension in the muscles. In addition, fear also brings physical changes of which we are not consciously aware. The digestive processes slow down, for example, and there might be a rise in blood pressure or a change in brain wave activity.

Apparently all types of emotion are accompanied by physical changes such as these, which put the body in a state of readiness for action.* If the emotion lasts for a short time, as is usually the case, the corresponding physical response is also of brief duration. When the emotion fades, the physical organism returns to normal.

Sometimes, however, the emotion persists for longer

---

*This is the principle on which the polygraph or lie detector works. It is assumed that if an individual tells a lie, he will experience fear, anxiety, or some other emotion. These emotions will be accompanied by physical changes which only the sensitive lie detector instruments will pick up.

periods of time. People who are constantly tense, hostile, anxious, worried, grieving, or otherwise emotionally upset, experience a prolonged physical arousal which, after a while, adversely influences their health. The physiological disorders (sometimes called psychosomatic reactions) are physical illnesses which are the direct result of prolonged emotional states.

The American Psychiatric Association classifies the psychophysiological disorders into several groupings. In *musculoskeletal* disorders the individual's emotional problems bring on backaches, muscle cramps, rheumatism or arthritis. *Respiratory* disorders are those in which there are psychologically caused breathing difficulties such as asthma, bronchitis or even hiccoughs. *Cardiovascular* disorders concern the work of the heart, and include high blood pressure, irregularities in the heart rate, and chest pains. *Gastrointestinal* disorders refer to problems connected with digestion. Peptic ulcers are the most widely known of these, but constipation, heartburn, colitis (a disease of the colon), and stomach upsets can also have an emotional cause. Other psychophysical symptoms include skin reactions such as acne or eczema, painful urination, menstrual disturbances, obesity, glandular malfunctioning, intense fatigue, migraine headaches, sterility, impotence, frigidity, and problems with vision and hearing.

It must be emphasized that while these conditions may come about as the result of emotional disturbances, they are not always emotionally caused. Ulcers, for example, may develop as a direct result of anxiety, but this does not mean that anxiety is the cause of all ulcers. A competent physician is the only person who is qualified to judge whether or not a physical condition is caused by some emotional pressure.

The prevention and treatment of psychosomatic symptoms and disorders are essentially the prevention and treatment of prolonged emotional stress. [17] To prevent or remove such stress is sometimes a long process which includes medical treatment for symptoms accompanied by psychotherapy and a learning of more appropriate ways to meet one's problems.

When the psychologically produced symptoms are treated alone, there isn't much long-term improvement; but when people receive adequate therapy, the chances are excellent that the symptoms will completely and permanently disappear.

## Special Symptoms

A number of bothersome symptoms sometimes begin in childhood and persist into adulthood. These symptoms do not necessarily indicate that an individual is seriously disturbed, but they do suggest that there are at least mild adjustment problems. Usually one symptom from the following list predominates: learning disturbances, sleep problems such as insomnia and sleepwalking, stuttering, thumbsucking, nail-biting, bed-wetting, excessive masturbation, lying, stealing or truancy.

These symptoms are most prevelent in childhood and sometimes they disappear spontaneously as the individual gets older, more self-confident, and more competent in dealing with the problems of living. When the special symptoms persist, a variety of treatment techniques may be used. Sometimes drugs or the use of various learning procedures can eliminate the undesirable behavior, and often the symptoms disappear when parents and others ignore them and stop making comments about them. At other times it is necessary to reduce tension in the environment and to treat the child in psychotherapy. The chances for improvement are very good.

## Transient Situational Disturbances
### CIVILIAN CATASTROPHES

In the summer of 1966 a group of tourists stood in line waiting for their turn to ride a cable car over a giant glacier in the French Alps. It was a clear beautiful day and for those riding in the cable cars the view was perfect. Suddenly a piece of metal snapped and three crowded cars crashed to the snow a hundred feet below. The rest of the cars were locked immediately into place by an automatic braking system. Then, for several hours, terrified passengers in crowded cars swayed suspended as they waited for rescuers to reach them and lower them to the ground below.

In reporting on this event, *Life* magazine pictured women being lowered from their cars and showed the scene on the ground following the rescue. Near one picture was the following caption: "Mountaineers comfort two sisters, uninjured but in hysterics after hours in a car which they expected to fall."

The behavior shown by these two women might be classified as transient and situational. It is termed "transient" because it is of short duration and will soon pass. It is "situational" because the behavior has come about as the result of an exceptionally stressful event or situation.

Temporary disturbances in behavior can occur following any number of stressful events. Accidents such as the one described above, car or plane crashes, floods, hurricanes, tornados, earthquakes and other severe weather conditions, fires, disasters at sea, bombings of civilian centers, a sudden death in the family, and assault or rape—all place people under intense stress which sometimes leads to a breakdown in behavior. At some time most church leaders will be called upon to minister to people showing transient reactions to such extreme situational stress.

There are at least three ways in which transient disorders differ from the more serious behavior disturbances. First, the individual usually has had no previous history of abnormality; second, the reaction doesn't last very long; and third, the abnormal behavior always occurs in response to a stressful situation.

People pass through three stages following a severely stressful event. In the *shock stage*, most persons are initially dazed,

150

stunned, bewildered and apathetic. The silence which reigned over Hiroshima immediately after the atomic bomb exploded might at least be partially explained by this shock reaction. Of course, all people do not react in the same way initially. Some people become panic-stricken while others are outwardly "calm, cool, and collected." The *suggestible stage* is next. The individual tends to be passive, suggestible, and willing to take directions from other people who are less affected than he. Often there is a concern for the welfare of others involved in the disaster, and sometimes there are inefficient attempts to help others. In the *recovery stage* the individual must gradually regain his equilibrium. This stage may last for many weeks and be characterized by behavior such as tension and anxiety, inability to sleep, difficulty in concentration, frequent nightmares concerning the stressful event, a desire to talk about the event over and over again, depression, grief, hostility, and sometimes a variety of physical symptoms.[18]

These three stages are well-illustrated in a report published by two psychiatrists who interviewed survivors shortly after they were picked up following the collision of the Swedish liner *Stockholm* with the Italian luxury liner *Andrea Doria.*

> "During the phase of initial shock the survivors acted as if they had been sedated. . .as though nature provided a sedation mechanism which went into operation automatically". During the phase of suggestibility "the survivors presented themselves for the most part as an amorphous mass of people tending to act passively and compliantly. They displayed psychomotor retardation, flattening of affect, somnolence (drowsiness) and in some instances, amnesia for data of personal identification. They were nonchalant and easily suggestible." During the stage of recovery, after the initial shock had worn off and the survivors had received aid, "they showed. . .an apparently compulsive need to tell the story again and again, with identical detail and emphasis."[19]

Why do people react in this way? Prior to the stress situation, the world seemed relatively safe, secure and predictable. Suddenly there was an abrupt change and the individual, jolted and sometimes stunned by intense anxiety, was unable to adjust immediately. He was forced to rely temporarily on the help and direction of others. During the recovery stage he had to overcome his anxiety and learn to take up life again in a world that may have changed.

Initial treatment consists of removing the individual from the stressful situation and giving him rest (brought on by drugs if necessary). Later the person is encouraged to talk about his experiences and to ventilate his feelings. He is given reassurance, encouragement and guidance as he returns to his regular activities. Sometimes he is encouraged to return to the activity that he was pursuing at the time of the disaster. The near-drowning victim, for example, is usually urged to enter the water again, and the auto accident victim is taken for another car ride. This is to build confidence and hopefully to prevent a lifetime of anxiety.

A pastor, hospital chaplain, or Christian friend can be supportive and encouraging during any of the stress-reaction stages. During the recovery stage, especially, the church worker can pray with the victim, read comforting passages of Scripture, provide a sympathetic ear as he ventilates about his experiences, and help him to deal with grief, guilt, or questions like "Why did it happen to me?"

For people who have been stable and well-adjusted prior to the catastrophe, chances for complete recovery are excellent.

COMBAT REACTIONS

Some of the most stressful situations that human beings ever face occur in times of war. The infantry soldier, for example, is exposed to constant rifle and machine gun fire. He experiences prolonged noise, miserable living conditions, long periods without sleep, and an awareness that sudden death or injury might come at any time. The airman must fly over hostile territory, realizing that he is in danger of being shot down. The seaman lives in cramped living quarters with the peril of death at sea. In each case there is helplessness, and no knowledge of when things will improve.

After being under such stress for a while, the military man may become irritable, hypersensitive, and unable to sleep. These are the first signs of a developing disorder. Later there is intense anxiety (this is the most common symptom), great fatigue, and sometimes depression. Frequently the serviceman feels guilty or experiences self-condemnation and feelings of failure. All of this may be accompanied by physical symptoms such as pain, stomach trouble, inability to walk, etc. These latter symptoms are often unconscious attempts to keep out of further trouble.

> Robert is a 20-year-old soldier who became increasingly anxious as his unit moved into a combat for the first time. While his own unit was not under attack, the knowledge that severe fighting was taking place in a not too distant area was enough to bring on severe trembling. When he moved close enough to hear the rattle of machine gun fire and the explosions of artillery shells, his trembling became uncontrollable. Finally, in complete terror, he became ill, vomited, and was unable to control his bladder and bowels. He wandered around the area in confusion until he was observed by a medical officer who had him returned to the rear. This severe anxiety reaction occurred even though the unit to which the soldier was assigned was never under direct fire. [20]

In combat situations most of the adjustment techniques that have been useful during civilian life are no longer of value. The relatively safe and predictable civilian world has been replaced by an environment of continual danger which one is helpless to control. Familiar surroundings and the encouragement of loved ones are far away. Instead there is a strange, new and unpleasant environment. Add to this the guilt feelings about killing which some men feel, the frequent contact with death, the lack of knowledge concerning the purposes or progress of the war, and the conflict between a desire for safety and a desire to "not let down your buddies," and it is perhaps easier to understand why some men develop combat disorders.

Many years ago it was thought that such men should be removed for hospital treatment far from the scene of battle. When men reached the relative security of the hospital, however, their symptoms often did not change. Since improvement would have meant return to combat, most men decided unconsciously that it was better and a great deal safer to be "sick" in a hospital and unfit for battle.

During World War II and in the Korean and Vietnam wars it was found to be more effective if treatment was given as near to the front lines as possible. Psychological casualties were given rest and sleep, often brought on by sedatives, an opportunity to ventilate feelings, supportive encouragement, and an attitude on the part of the treatment staff that the man would soon be back helping his buddies in the battle. As a result of such treatment, many men were able to rejoin their units after a few days and only the most severe cases were sent from the scene.

There is good chance for recovery from combat reactions if the individual showed good adjustment in civilian life, is treated near the front lines, and is treated shortly after the appearance of his symptoms. Of course, it should be remembered that 90 percent of military men never require any treatment for combat reactions. This is probably due in part to military selection procedures which reject those who are likely to develop behavior disorders, and in part to training which does much to prepare men for the stress of battle.

## CHRONIC SITUATIONAL STRESS REACTIONS

The civilian and combat reactions described above usually occur in the presence of stress which is intense but of relatively short duration. But stress sometimes continues for months or years. Chronic stress reactions are abnormalities in behavior which occur as a result of this more persistent environmental pressure. While a number of these reactions might be considered, we will mention only three: reactions to life periods, reactions to reduced environmental stimulation, and reactions to brainwashing.

*Reaction to life periods.* Each period of life is characterized by special stresses which persist for a few years and then are replaced by other pressures. In childhood, for example, rejection by parents, frequent physical illness, lack of athletic or academic skills, or an inability to get along with teachers, are examples of prolonged stress which may create adjustment difficulties. Teenage and college years bring a new series of pressures as the individual must adjust to the pressure of physical changes, new social expectations, and the need to find a niche in life. In adulthood there are sometimes prolonged pressures connected with one's work, marriage, finances or health. Then when one reaches old age, there are pressures connected with retirement, changes in economic status, health problems, etc. When the individual is removed from prolonged stresses such as these, the reaction often disappears spontaneously, although sometimes brief counseling can be beneficial in teaching new attitudes and more efficient ways of behaving.

*Reactions to reduced environmental stimulation.* Most of us have at some time experienced boredom and loneliness. When we have nothing to do, or when other people are not around, we sometimes get depressed, unhappy or restless and may even show signs of abnormality. This was the experience of Admiral Byrd who lived alone for several months in the cold Antartic in 1938. Adventuresome people who have made long, monotonous trips in little boats have reported hallucinations and abnormal reactions as a result of the lack of changing stimulation, and even deaf people or those who are confined to wheelchairs and iron lungs sometimes react with anxiety, disorientation and hallucinations because of their reduced contact with the environment. These observations have caused a number of psychologists to conclude that in order to function effectively, each of us must receive a certain amount of changing stimulation from the environment around us. [21]

A few years ago some psychologists at McGill University conducted an experiment to see what would happen if the amount of environmental stimulation was sharply reduced. [22] Student volunteers were paid to do nothing for as long as they could. They were blindfolded with transluscent goggles in order to reduce visual stimulation, wore long cuffs over their hands to prevent touching, and remained alone in a room which was partially soundproofed to reduce noise. Apart from eating and toilet times, the subjects were expected to lie quietly on a comfortable bed. In spite of the financial incentives, most subjects could not endure this experiment for any more than a couple of days. The reduction in stimulation brought extreme behavior changes such as hallucinations, confusion, impaired thinking, and childish emotional responses. All of these symptoms disappeared when normal stimulation returned.

*Reactions to brainwashing.* In 1953 a psychologist named Edgar Schein interviewed prisoners of war shortly after they had been released from Communist prison camps. The prisoners reported that they had all been treated in a somewhat similar way. After almost unbelievable physical hardships, they were subjected to long periods of questioning and indoctrination. Letters from home were withheld or censored. Newspapers and other contacts with the outside world were withdrawn. Spies lived with the prisoners, so no one ever knew who could be trusted or who was a friend of the captors. The prisoners lived in such a state of uncertainty that even mealtimes were irregular.

For many persons this perpetual state of anxiety was unbearable, and a stage of crisis and breakdown occurred, usually after about six months.

The crisis usually starts with hysteria and sobbing at night, which go on during the small group meeting the next day and are immediately discussed. . . .The crisis usually comes at about the same time for all the members of a small group. Apparently the breakdown of one of the members launches a chain reaction. . . .In some cases, of course, it is much more evident than in others. . . .One former trainee claimed that a fifth of the trainees broke down completely and some ended as "babbling maniacs." [23]

Here, as in other transient situations, the reactions often clear up rapidly when the individual is removed from the stress situation. Sometimes, however, the released prisoner has difficulty in making a readjustment to civilian life. Some experience chronic fatigue and physical disabilities for many months. Others get into trouble with the law because they give vent to their long pent-up hostility feelings. In many there is a lowered ability to withstand stress of any kind. In spite of these variations in adjustment, however, follow-up studies indicate that most prisoners of war are able to make satisfactory readjustments to civilian life. [24]

## SUMMARY

This lengthy chapter summarizes most of the common abnormal reactions. We began with a consideration of *brain disorders*—those abnormalities in behavior which result from a diseased, damaged or destroyed brain. Then we discussed the *psychoses.* These are severe mental disorders "marked by symptoms that a layman most readily attributes to a deranged mind: grossly disturbed, bizarre and unconventional behavior, irrationality, conspicuous mental or emotional abnormality." [25] Most of these patients must be admitted to mental hospitals.

*Neurosis*, another category of disorders, refers to behavior which is characterized by anxiety, tension, physical symptoms, rigidity, unhappiness, and strained interpersonal relations. The neurotic lives and manages to get along in society, but he depends on his symptoms to help him deal with persistent stressful situations. Also living in the society are people with *personality disorders*. They have certain characteristics—such as immaturity or a dislike for others—that influence their whole way of life and cause them to be thought of as odd or eccentric. When stress gives rise to physical illness, we have *psychophysiological reactions.*

*The transient situational disorders* are temporary responses to excessive environmental stress. They include civilian reactions to tragedy, combat disorders, and the abnormalities that occur when people are subjected to brainwashing or other prolonged periods of stress.

Most of the disorders that have been discussed in this chapter are popularly labeled "mental illness." In the next chapter we turn to a group of disorders which may be just as disturbing to the individual but which are characterized by behavior which the society considers to be antisocial.

# 5

# Alcoholism, Drug Addiction and Social Deviance

In any society, there are a number of people, including alcoholics, drug addicts, sex deviates, criminals, and juvenile delinquents, who behave in ways which are antisocial. These people are in contact with reality, they rarely show the symptoms of neurosis or psychosis, and they seldom give the appearance of being "mentally ill." More often they turn up in jails instead of in mental hospitals, and if they do seek psychological help it is usually in response to pressure from their families or the courts.

Because of their deviant behavior, these people place a great financial burden on society. They cause untold anguish for their own families and for those whom they willingly or unwillingly victimize. Jesus was criticized for associating with these social outcasts and their victims, but He clearly cared for them (Mt. 9:10-13; Lk. 19:1-10; 10:30-37). The Scriptures direct contemporary Christians to have a similar concern (Gal. 6:2, 10; Ja. 1:22, 27). To do this effectively, the church leader must first have an understanding of the various antisocial disorders discussed in this chapter.

## ALCOHOLISM

After the flood, Noah turned to farming and began by planting a vineyard (Gen. 9:20). According to an ancient Hebrew legend, it was about this time that the devil offered to help and poured the blood of a sheep, a lion, a monkey and a pig at the roots of the vines. As a result of the devil's actions, when a mild and inoffensive sheeplike man begins to drink the fruit of the vine, he behaves like a lion—proud and self-confident. Later he chatters and scurries about like a foolish monkey; and if he continues to drink, he falls to the ground and wallows like a pig in the filth. Of the over seventy million people in the United States who drink, only a small minority fall and wallow in alcoholism. Most people drink in moderation and find that alcohol is both relaxing and a reliever of tension. Unfortunately, it is not always possible to predict in advance which drinkers will become addicted to alcohol and which will not.

Alcohol does not influence behavior until it passes through the walls of the stomach or intestines and into the bloodstream. This process is speeded up considerably if the drinking proceeds at a fast rate, if there is a large concentration of alcohol in the drinks, or if there is no food in the stomach to absorb the alcohol. Once in the bloodstream, alcohol displaces the oxygen in the red blood cells and has a numbing effect on the brain. When the concentration of alcohol in the blood is one-twentieth of 1 percent, the average person feels relaxed, free from worry, calm, unafraid of the future, and "on top of his problems." Soon, however, he loses the ability to be self-critical or to hold some of his impulses in check. A concentration of one-tenth of 1 percent influences the motor and visual areas of the brain so that the drinker staggers, has trouble with his speech, and has reduced visual ability. At two-tenths of 1 percent, there is often nausea and complete loss of emotional control. Later the individual passes out, and if the concentration rises above half of 1 percent, death may result. These figures are averages since the effects of alcohol differ considerably from person to person.

It has been roughly estimated that of every fifteen people who take a drink, one becomes an alcoholic. That person is characterized by a compulsion to drink alcoholic beverages excessively even though the drinking is harmful for him, inability to control his drinking, deterioration of his competence in mental, emotional, physical, family, job or social areas, and use of alcohol as a means of handling serious personality problems.[1]

## DEVELOPMENT OF ALCOHOLISM

As his alcoholism develops, the individual passes through a number of predictable stages, illustrated in Figure 5-1. It should be emphasized that these downward steps represent the typical sequence through which males pass in becoming addicted. Not all of these symptoms occur in all cases, and the order and age of their appearance may vary. In addition, there are sex differences. Women go through these stages more quickly than men, and as alcoholics they engage in more antisocial behavior and a greater number of suicide attempts. In spite of these individual variations, however, the information in Figure 5-1 can be helpful to the church leader since it enables him both to identify prospective alcoholics and to determine the stage to which the disorder has progressed.

Don, age 26, is the only son of a successful east coast businessman and his wife. When he was a baby, Don's parents separated and the responsibility for his upbringing fell to his mother. She was a Christian lady who faithfully took her son to church and tried to maintain a good home, even though it was necessary for her to work full time and to leave her son in the care of a baby sitter. When he became a teenager, Don was introduced to alcohol by some of his buddies and during his last year in high school he had his first experience of getting drunk.

At his mother's urging, Don enrolled in a Christian college and successfully completed his course of study, graduating with a degree in business administration. He continued to drink regularly during his college years, however, especially when the pressures of school got intense. Apparently Don's classmates knew nothing of his drinking and in his last year he became engaged to a pastor's daughter who was also a

161

**Pre-Alcoholic Symptom Phase**
Periodic drinking to obtain relief from tension
Getting drunk (18.8)
Increase in tolerance

**Prodromal Phase**
First blackout (brief period of amnesia, without loss of consciousness. There is no later memory of one's actions while drinking (25.2)
Sneaking drinks, preoccupation with drinking, gulping the first few drinks, guilt feelings, avoiding any discussions of drinking (25.9)
Increase in frequency of blackouts

**Crucial Phase**
Loss of control over drinking (one drink starts a chain reaction so that the individual cannot stop on a given occasion until he is too drunk or too sick to drink any more)
Persistent (but futile) attempts to stop or control drinking
Grandiose and aggressive behavior, accompanied by feelings of remorse
Making excuse (alibis) to explain away his drinking (29.2)
Begin to lose friends and outside interests
Morning drinks ("eye-openers") to help one face the day (29.9)
Neglect of food
Work and money troubles leading to loss of job (30.9)
Decrease in sex drive accompanied by increased jealousy
Drinking alone, accompanied by increased isolation as thoughts and behavior center more and more around alcohol (31.2)
Physical and moral deterioration
Anti-social behavior (31.3)

**Alcoholic Phase**
Benders (prolonged bouts of intoxication which may last for several days, often followed by attempts to "get on the wagon" (31.8)
Increasing fears and tremors (32.9)
Deterioration in thinking
Drinking with inferiors — ignoring social level or personal characteristics
Deep resentment and remorse (33.1)
Willingness to drink anything, including rubbing alcohol
Obsession with drinking
Vague feelings of a need for religion (35.7)
Decreased tolerance (It is possible to get drunk on a smaller amount of liquor)
Alibis are cast aside
Admit to self, the inability to control drinking (38.1)
Admit to others, the inability to control drinking (39.5)
Hit bottom (Usually there is malnutrition, sometimes accompanied by delerium tremens, hallucinations, and liver disease. Drinking often occurs in an attempt to control the symptoms of drinking. This is a vicious cycle)

*Figure 5-1*

## Steps to Alcohol Addiction*

*Based on M. M. Glatt, "Group Therapy in Alcoholism," *British Journal of Addiction* 54 (1957) and E. M. Jellinek, "Phases in the Drinking History of Alcoholism," *Quarterly Journal of Studies on Alcohol* (1946) and "Phases of Alcohol Addiction," *Quarterly Journal of Studies on Alcohol* 13 (1952): 673-78.

Figures in parentheses indicate the average (mean) age at which behavior first occurs.

member of the graduating class. They were married shortly after graduation and moved to the midwest where Don had been hired by a large business corporation.

When faced with the pressures of selling, Don's drinking increased. He would often take a customer to lunch, start drinking, and never get back to his office. When he came for counseling at the insistence of his wife, Don reported that he had been involved in several accidents because of his drinking. In the most recent of these he apparently rammed into a tree on a lonely country road. Early the next morning he "woke up" and discovered himself sitting alone in his car with no idea where he was. Because of these accidents, his wife had begun calling bars on those evenings when her husband was not home for dinner. When she would find him, she would make her way to the bar and then bring him home.

Afraid of the reaction of her parents, Don's wife suffered alone and refused to tell anyone of her husband's problem. Their marriage was degenerating and there were frequent arguments—usually about Don's drinking. After a drinking bout, he was often very apologetic and remorseful but in spite of his promises to quit, his drinking behavior always started again. On Sundays the couple attended church, but they had no friends in the congregation and did not tell the pastor about their problem.

## CAUSES OF ALCOHOLISM

Although there has been considerable research on the problem, the basic causes of alcoholism are still unknown. Since the Bible condemns excessive use of alcohol (Pr. 20:1; 23:20, 29-35; Is. 5:11; Hab. 2:15; Lk. 21:34; Ro. 13:13; Eph. 5:18), many Christians have assumed that alcoholism is really caused by sin. While there is much truth in this conclusion, studies have shown that physiological, psychological and social issues are also very important.

Although people differ in the ways that their bodies react to alcohol, there is presently no conclusive evidence to suggest that some people are biologically more vulnerable than others. Excessive drinkers often become physically depend-dent on liquor, but this may be more the result of learning than of innate physical susceptibility.

Most heavy drinkers are people who use alcohol to relieve anxiety and to shut out the stresses of the world around. Research has shown that alcoholics are frequently immature, insecure, unhappy, lonely people who come from homes where authoritarianism, a worship of success, excessive moralism, and overt rejection of the children are common.[2] The drinker may realize that his heavy consumption of alcohol may lead to sickness or trouble with his family and employer, but thoughts about the future are not enough to offset the more immediate relief that comes from drinking.

Of course a lot of people have problems, so why is it that some become alcoholics while others do not? The answer seems to be that people turn to alcohol for one or a combination of four reasons. First, there is the attitude and example of parents. When parents use alcohol to reduce tension, children tend to do the same. Second, there is the issue of availability. Alcohol is easily acquired and for this reason it is frequently used. During prohibition, when liquor was harder to get, the rate of drinking dropped significantly. Cultural attitudes provide a third reason. When a society looks with favor on drinking, there is a greater amount of alcoholism. In France and the United States, for example, drinking is generally accepted and alcoholism is high. By way of contrast, in Jewish, Muslim and Mormon communities, alcoholism is very low because these cultural groups frown on excessive drinking. Fourth, there is the nonavailability of alternate ways to relieve anxiety. Alcoholism is more likely to occur when there is no other way to dull the tensions of life. The recent increase in drug use may reflect the tendency of people to pursue a way of escape which at least appears to be better than alcohol. It remains to be seen whether an increase in drug abuse is accompanied by a decline in alcoholism.

## TREATMENT OF ALCOHOLISM

How can alcoholism be treated? The alcoholic must first be stopped from drinking. This is primarily a medical procedure in which the patient is taken off alcohol completely and given rest, nourishing food, and drugs—all of which help to build up his physical strength. Since the "dry" alcoholic can never again drink socially or in a controlled way, he must then be helped to completely abstain from drinking.

Various approaches have been used to accomplish this goal, including moral exhortation in which the drinker is urged to stop, conditioning in which alcohol is paired with a nausea-producing drug so that the individual subsequently avoids liquor for fear of getting sick, rescue-mission preaching and rehabilitation programs, group and individual psychotherapy which seeks to deal with the patient's underlying problems and anxieties, and the program of Alcoholics Anonymous. While all of these work to some extent, the first is clearly least effective and the last appears to be the most successful treatment procedure.

Alcoholics Anonymous (AA) was established in 1935 and now has about 300,000 members in countries all over the world.* These men and women keep sober by helping other alcoholics, by living their lives in the present (one day at a time), and by not moaning over the past or worrying about the future. At AA meetings they have a friendly, noncondemning attitude, and sincerely desire to help one another. Although the group is not allied with any sect, denomination or other group, there is a strong religious (not necessarily Christian) emphasis. Members strive to follow the "Twelve Steps" (see Table 5-1), and meetings are often opened or closed with prayer.

---

*Telephone directories in most major communities list a number to call if one wants to contact local AA members.

*Table 5-1*

## Alcoholics Anonymous' Twelve Steps to Sobriety

1. We must admit that we are powerless over alcohol—that our lives have become unmanageable.

2. We must come to believe that only a Power greater than ourselves can restore us to sanity.

3. We must decide to turn our will and our lives over to the care of God *as we understand Him*.

4. We must make a searching and fearless moral inventory of ourselves.

5. We must admit to God, to ourselves, and to another human being the exact nature of our wrongs.

6. We are entirely ready for God to remove all these defects of character.

7. We humbly ask Him to remove our shortcomings.

8. We make a list of all the persons we have harmed, and are willing to make amends to them all.

9. We make amends to such people wherever possible, except where to do so would cause injury to them or to others.

10. We continue to take personal inventory and when we are wrong promptly admit it.

11. We seek through prayer and meditation to improve our conscious contact with God *as we understand Him*, praying only for knowledge of His will for us and power to carry that out.

12. Having had a spiritual awakening as a result of these steps, we try to carry this message to alcoholics and to practice these principles in all of our affairs.

The church leader is in a unique position to be of help both to the alcoholic and to his family. This is a frustrating, time-consuming task, however, which requires a great deal of patience and understanding.

In working with the excessive drinker, it is important to be accepting and to help him to face the reality of his problem.[3] There is no value in scolding, preaching, ridiculing, or reminding him of his failures. Instead, he should be permitted to talk about his feelings of failure or remorse, and to confess these to the counselor and to God. The drinker should be helped to deal with his problems and to learn to stand on his own. To achieve this end, all excuses, babying, pitying or encouraging excessive dependency should be avoided. It helps if the drinker can be in touch with other alcoholics (such as those in AA) and if he can get competent medical and psychological treatment. In addition to this, the church leader can point to what are undoubtedly the drinker's greatest resources—the love, concern, and help of a God who cares about individual men and women.

The alcoholic's family also needs considerable support and encouragement. As the drinker sinks into alcoholism, the family experiences great stress.[4] First there are internal family dissensions over the drinking, often accompanied by attempts to deny that a serious problem is developing. The family tries to control the drinking and to hide the problem from the outside world. As the drinking gets worse, the family begins to withdraw from social contacts. Eventually the nondrinking spouse takes over, and sometimes the family breaks up. By listening, sharing facts about alcoholism, and being a sincere, understanding friend, the church leader can be of great help to these families. The drinker's relatives should not be pampered or encouraged to wallow in self-pity, but they should be stimulated to remain socially active. In this respect the whole church can be an understanding, supportive and accepting community. It is also

167

wise to encourage participation in the family groups which are connected with A.A. In addition, the relatives of alcoholics, like the drinkers themselves, can find support in the words of Scripture and in the knowledge that concerned Christians are praying.

Counselors are sometimes surprised to discover that when drinking stops, a whole new set of family problems arises. Over the years a family develops certain standards and ways of behaving which, in the alcoholic's home, may involve treating the drinker as an irresponsible child. If an alcoholic father or mother stops drinking and wants to participate as a responsible member of the family, everyone in the home has to readjust. A wife, for example, who has been the breadwinner and head of the house, may have great difficulty in giving this role back to her spouse. The family may need considerable guidance and encouragement as they learn a whole new way of living.

PREVENTION OF ALCOHOLISM

In the mid '60s, the National Institute of Mental Health financed a one million dollar study on the problems of alcoholism.[5] To prevent excessive drinking, the report concluded, the legal drinking age should be lowered, drinking in moderation should be made more acceptable, and young people should be taught how to drink—at home, at school events, and at church functions. This proposal, which unfortunately was endorsed by several influential church leaders, condones the very factors which encourage anxious people to turn to alcohol: increased use of liquor in the home, increased availability, and greater social acceptance of drinking.

Surely it is much more realistic to deglamorize drinking; to encourage parents to avoid excessive use of alcohol; to work with the children of alcoholics (30 percent of whom follow the parental example and develop a drinking problem); to work at preventing authoritarianism, success-worship, moralizing and overt rejection in the home; to counsel people with personal anxieties and insecurities; and to be alert to the signs of alcoholism so that we can encourage early treatment.[6] All of these can be tasks and responsibilities for the church leader, and he can also use what is probably the best preventive—encouraging people not to start drinking in the first place.

## DRUG USE AND ADDICTION

In our modern society the use of drugs is almost universal; practically everyone at some time seeks relief from pain, tension and boredom by depending on the influence of some drug. While most people are content to stick with aspirin, caffeine, nicotine, or the occasional use of alcohol, others take stronger drugs and use them in increasing quantities.

Table 5-2 lists some of the more common types of drugs. In considering these it is important that we distinguish between addiction and habituation. *Addiction* is characterized by an overpowering desire to continue using the drug, a tendency over a period of time to increase the dosage, a psychological and physical dependence on the drug, and great stress (withdrawal symptoms) when use of the drug is stopped. In *habituation* there is desire for the drug but no compulsive craving, the dosage remains the same over a period of time, there is no real dependence on the drug, and withdrawal does not cause any significant disturbance. Usually people become habituated to caffeine but addicted to drugs like morphine or heroin.*

With the widespread use of drugs there have also come a number o. misconceptions about addiction. While there are exceptions to each of the following, it is generally incorrect to conclude that addicts always appear degenerate, that withdrawal is always a horrible experience, that addicts entice children to use drugs, that the excessive drug user is violent or a sex fiend, that addiction is incurable, or that

---

*This is not *always* true since some people do become addicted to caffiene or nicotine, and show all of the characteristics of addiction (E. Rosen and I. Gregory, *Abnormal Psychology*).

addiction can be eliminated by imprisonment or the exercise of willpower.[7] Drug users, like nonusers, have different personalities. They react differently when under the influence of a drug, and they show different susceptibility to addiction.

The most common effects of the various drugs are listed as part of Table 5-2. In spite of these different symptoms, there are some general clues that may indicate drug use. These include (1) a decrease in communication so that the person talks less and has fewer interactions with others; (2) extremes of energy such as a decline in performance at school and work, or a tendency to be highly energetic and jumpy; (3) a change in appetite (depending on the drug, there may be a sharp increase or a decline in appetite); (4) the wearing of sunglasses; (5) sudden personality change, such as an increase in irritability, suspicion, aggression or confusion; (6) sloppier dress accompanied by body and breath odor; (7) increased difficulty waking up in the morning; (8) mysterious phone calls which may come from a pusher; (9) physical problems such as diarrhea, nausea or headaches; (10) needle marks on the body; (11) a decline in moral values; and (12) either very wide or very narrow pupils of the eyes.[8]

## CAUSES OF DRUG ADDICTION

It is during periods of sickness that most of us have our first and perhaps only experience with the more powerful drugs. Physicians are very alert to the dangers of medications, however, and usually are careful to prevent their patients from developing addictions. It is more common, therefore, for drug addicts—like alcoholics—to be taking drugs voluntarily and at times when they are not physically sick. There are several reasons why people do this.

*Group pressure and curiosity.* Young people, especially teenagers, are curious and very conscious of the opinions of their peers. To be accepted by the group, it is often necessary to dress, act, talk, and even think alike. By refusing to conform, the young person risks rejection and a loss in status; so if the "kids at school" are experimenting with drugs, alcohol and sex, most young people want to "go along with the crowd," just "to see what it's like." For many of them, such experimentation is temporary and disappears often after one experience. But for others, yielding to group pressure is the first step to drug abuse and addiction.

*Rebellion.* In growing up, teenagers like to express their independence of adult authority and social norms. Reckless ,driving, juvenile delinquency, and other "antiestablishment" behavior—including the taking of illegal drugs—are often effective, albeit immature, ways to express rebellion. After eighteen, this behavior tends to disappear in all but those maladjusted people who learn to cope with unpleasant reality by continued reliance on the drugs.

*To avoid boredom and provide novelty.* This probably accounts for use of the so-called mind-expanding or psychologenic drugs. In many people today, life is boring, meaningless and futile. Distressed over the current international situation and frustrated with the establishment, many thinking people turn to drugs as an escape from futility and an opportunity for excitement. For these people, life is not characterized by a philosophy of "Eat, drink and be merry, for tomorrow we die." Instead, the cry is "Turn on, tune in, and drop out for tomorrow ... ?"

*Emotional immaturity.* As he grows toward adulthood, the individual must move away from parental dependence. He must learn self-discipline, responsibility, the ability to make independent decisions, and the patience to postpone immediate pleasure-seeking for the sake of advancing long-range goals. Such maturing is often very painful. It is really much easier to remain immature, self-centered, self-indulging and irresponsible. Research suggests that many drug addicts are among those who have refused to grow up.[9] By using drugs, the individual avoids facing responsibility

171

# Classification of Some Major Drugs*

| Drug Class | Sample Drugs | Slang Names |
|---|---|---|
| **SEDATIVES AND HYPNOTICS** | *Narcotics*<br>—opium<br>—morphine<br>  synthetic substitutes for<br>—morphine<br>—demerol<br>—methadone etc.<br>—heroin<br>—codeine etc. | dreamer, M<br><br><br>snow, stuff, junk<br>schoolboy |
| | *Barbituates*<br>—phenobarbital<br>—nembutal<br>—seconal, etc. | sleeping pills, barbs, goofballs, red birds, yellow jackets, blue heavens |
| | *Bromide*<br>—bromo seltzer<br>—potassium bromide | |
| | *Alcohol* | booze |
| **STIMULANTS** | *Cocaine* | Leaf, snow, speedballs (when mixed with heroin) |
| | *Amphetamines*<br>—benzedrine<br>—dexedrine<br>—methedrine | bennies, co-pilots, footballs, pep pills, hearts |
| | *Methamphetamine*<br>  (methedrine) | speed, crystal |
| | *Nicotine, Caffeine* | tobacco, coffee and tea |
| **HALLUCINOGENS** | LSD<br>—Mescaline (peyote)<br>—Bufotenine | acid |
| | Marijuana | pot, grass, weed, joints, sticks, reefers, muggles, mooters, mu, Mary Jane, etc. |
| **PSYCHO-THERAPEUTICS** | *Antipsychotic*<br>—reserpine<br>—chlorpromazine | tranquilizers |
| | *Antianxiety*<br>—meprobromate<br>  (equanil, miltown)<br>—phenobarbital | tranquilizers |
| | *Antidepressant*<br>—imipramine<br>  (tofrinal) | |
| **ANESTHETICS** | Chloroform<br>Analgesics<br>Paralytic<br>Local anesthetics | |

*From American Social Health Association (1968), T. L. Duncan, *Understanding and Helping the Narcotic Addict*, and Jarville (1967).

172

# Table 5-2

| General Effects | Evidence of Addiction | | Availability** |
|---|---|---|---|
| | emotional | physical | |
| Relieve pain, cause mental and physical numbing and inactivity (sedation), produce sleep (hypnosis). Often used to treat mental stress, insomnia, anxiety. Heavier doses can produce coma or death from respiratory failure. | yes | yes | P |
| Induces sleep and calming. Small doses make the user relaxed, sociable, good humored. Larger doses make him sluggish, gloomy, sometimes quarrelsome, with an appearance of drunkenness (but with no odor of alcohol). High dosage often produces coma and death from respiratory failure. | yes | yes | P |
| Induce sleep and calming. | yes | no | A |
| See discussion of alcohol in text | yes | yes | A |
| Stimulates central nervous system to produce excitement, alertness, increased initiative, activity and confidence, elevation in mood and freedom from fatigue. Overuse may lead to jumpiness, hyperactivity, heart disorders, convulsions, paranoia. | yes | no | P |
| | yes | no | P |
| Sleep and calming. Also can lead to extreme restlessness and irritability. Overdose is often fatal ("speed kills"). | yes | no | P |
| Very mild stimulation. Larger and prolonged dosages of nicotine can produce cancer, respiratory disorders. | yes | in some cases | A |
| Produce change in mood, thinking and behavior. May produce a psychotic like state with delusions, hallucinations, irrational behavior and distortions of sense perceptions. Drugs have little therapeutic value and sometimes precipitate psychosis or damage chromosomes. | yes | no | I |
| Effects are unpredictable, but usually produces feelings of pleasure, euphoria, relaxation, hilarity, perceptual distortions, and self-confidence. Often there is a loss of restraints so that the user engages in behavior which is dangerous to himself and others. Thought to be a stepping-stone to use of more dangerous drugs. | yes | no | I |
| Used to treat psychological disorders. Similar to sedatives. | yes | no | P |
| Control insomnia, reduce mental stress, produce relaxation. | yes | yes | P |
| Stimulate depressed patients to become more active and interested in activities. Diminishes lethargy and apathy. | yes | no | P |
| Used in medicine to deaden pain during medical procedures. | no | no | P |
| | yes | yes | P |
| | no | no | P |
| | no | no | P |

**P—On recommendation of a physician
I—Illegal to manufacture and distribute (except for research purposes).
A—Available without prescription

but at the same time is able to experience feelings of pleasure and superiority.

Why do some people refuse to grow up? The reasons can often be found at home. If the parents are overprotecting (shielding their child from the stresses of life), overdominating (so that they set impossibly high standards), or underdominating (so that the child has few demands placed on him), the child never learns to face the stresses of life.[10] Often well-meaning parents in good homes do a disservice to their children because the offspring are never "trained up" and given experience "in the way they should go." As a result, there is a turning to drugs in place of maturity.

*Relief from anxiety.* Some people who live busy lives and have a high desire for status but a fear of failure, use drugs to help meet the stress of life. Nurses, doctors and other professional people often fit into this category.

> One physician was starting a new practice. He was working long hours trying to establish a reputation for himself. Before long, he became fatigued, but having the strong need to prove himself (which may have been anxiety due to lack of self-confidence), he began to take stimulants to keep going. Through continual use, he became so stimulated he could not rest. To rest, he began to take depressant drugs, thinking they would bring him back down to normal. He seldom could make the combination just right. He would get too much depressant and soon would have to take a stimulant, then more depressant, then more stimulant. The pressure of trying to keep a balance between his drugs took so much energy and produced so much anxiety that he began to slip in his practice of medicine. As this failed, he would increase his medication. Eventually he became completely frustrated, was unable to continue, and required hospitalization.[11]

People such as this physician have no desire for "kicks." They more often become habituated than addicted, and they are very sensitive to the reactions of other people.

Nevertheless, these professionals sometimes become addicts who are dependent on drugs.

*Expression of delinquency.* Some persons who have antisocial tendencies take drugs as another manifestation of their delinquency. Why these people become delinquents in the first place is considered later in the chapter.

People first take drugs for a number of reasons, but apparently it is only the immature and the insecure who continue to use drugs. Since the addict can no longer tolerate the drug's absence, he is often forced to engage in criminal acts in order to get money to pay for his daily supply. Thus his life is a vicious, frantic circle of struggling to get more drugs before the effects of the last ingestion wear off.

## TREATMENT OF DRUG ADDICTION

As with alcoholism, the drug addict's treatment consists of two phases: getting him off the drug, and helping him to stay off. Withdrawal from drugs is often distressing and physically painful, but medical treatment can do much to alleviate the symptoms. As a result, withdrawal is sometimes no worse than a case of the flu. [12]

Keeping a person off drugs is much more difficult, for most addicts who are treated in hospitals become addicted again within a few months. Narcotics Anonymous has helped some people, but in general it has been less successful than Alcoholics Anonymous. More effective are self-help programs, such as Synanon and Daytop Village where former addicts live together in a highly organized community. Since addicts are assumed to be immature, the philosophy is to treat new members of the community like little children in an attempt to help them grow up. The treatment is often harsh, but the results are encouraging. [13] Religious programs have also been somewhat successful. Teen Challenge, for example, provides a living situation with rigid rules and a strong belief that drugs must be replaced by faith in and increased dependence on Jesus Christ. [14]

175

In view of the general ineffectiveness of the treatment, it is probably true that prevention is the best treatment. This can take several forms:

*Reduce availability.* In the opinion of some people, drugs should be legalized and made more available. Illegally produced drugs are alreay available to any person who wants them, including high school students, but it would still seem that there will be less experimentation if there is less availability.

*Provide accurate information.* Young people especially should be alerted to the dangers of drugs. Such information should be presented accurately, honestly, without reliance on sensationalism, and (where possible) by a person who is somewhat the same age as the audience. In education programs, care should be taken not to lump all drugs together. Some drugs, like heroin, are clearly addictive, but this may not be true of LSD or marijuana. Some drugs may be very harmful, but others may have less of an influence on the user. The educator, including the Christian educator, who doesn't know his drugs *well*, will not be heard.

*Strengthen the family.* The homelife of addicts is often characterized by lack of warmth, lack of parental concern or involvement with the children, strife and hostility, overprotection, overdomination *or* underdomination. In addition, there is often a domineering overpowering mother and a weak (or absent) father.[15] In contrast, cohesive families which are characterized by love, security and guidance more often produce secure, maturing children who have no need to cover their immaturity with drugs. The church, more than any other influence in society, can guide in the building and strengthening of family solidarity.

*Guide immature and insecure young people.* Helping people to become mature is clearly a parental responsibility, but sometimes the church and school must help. Drug addicts often have a great desire to grow up, to belong, and to develop self-confidence.[16] Through counseling and the various church activities, church leaders can speed along this process.

*Eliminate the spiritual vacuum.* For most addicts, drugs meet a psychological and spiritual need. By rejecting and ignoring God, men often feel empty and their lives are boring and meaningless. For such people, drugs fill the void.

It is interesting that some drug users have developed religious cults or turned to the contemplative religions of the Far East. By embracing man-made religion, however, these people have settled for second best. Real meaning, purpose and joy in life come only to the person who submits his life to the lordship and control of Jesus Christ. Introducing men to Christ is clearly a responsibility, not only for the church leader, but for every believer.

## SEXUAL DEVIATIONS

"In less than half a century sex in American life has rocketed from the unmentionable to a topic of almost obsessive public concern. The management of sexual activity. . .has become a high priority preoccupation for vast segments of our society."[17] When this "management of sexual activity" deviates from what is socially acceptable, we say that the behavior is sexually perverted or deviate.

Many people who are suffering with behavior abnormalities show deviant sex behavior. Neurotics, psychotics, retarded persons, alcoholics and addicts, for example, frequently engage in sexual activities which are socially unacceptable. As used by psychologists, however, the term "sexual deviate" is restricted to people who obtain sexual satisfaction in socially disapproved ways, but who are otherwise free from behavior abnormalities.

To a large extent the society determines what is deviate. Behavior which is considered perverse and unacceptable in one country or social group, for example, may be acceptable someplace else. Prostitution is licensed in Holland but illegal in Canada; homosexuality is legal in Britain but

177

a violation of the law in most of the United States. "Adult" films such as *I, a Woman* or *I Am Curious Yellow* (and *Blue*), are widely accepted in America but considered criminal in most Iron Curtain countries. Even within our society there are variations. Deep kissing is generally approved by those in the upper socioeconomic classes, but considered perverse by those with lower economic status and less education.[18] Some people believe that holding hands is immoral, but for others almost any kind of sexual behavior is acceptable, providing it is "motivated by love."

In general, the sexual deviations can be classified into four major categories. These are variations in the *amount* of sexual activity or interest, in the *way* in which impulses are gratified, in the choice of the sexual *object*, and in the *location* or setting where the sexual activity takes place. The prevalence of these various deviations is hard to determine since few people are willing to talk about their own sex behavior and even fewer want to discuss their sexual deviations. Kinsey and his co-workers concluded that approximately 70 percent of American men and "some lesser number of. . .females, engage in at least some 'perverse' sexual behavior at some time between adolescence and old age."[19] Even though this estimate seems high, it suggests that in most church congregations, there are at least a few people who engage in the deviations described below.

*Deviation in amount of interest and activity.* Within the normal population there are wide variations in the desire for sexual activity. Some people are so concerned about sex that their thinking, conversation, jokes, interests and reading are almost exclusively concerned with this subject. As might be expected, many (but not all) of these people engage in frequent sexual activity. While this may have a physical cause, it is more probable that such persons are unconsciously in need of love, attention, and opportunities to prove that they are sexually adequate.

At the opposite extreme are people who have an unusually low interest in sex—an attitude which often results from fear of the sex act, or the view that sex is dirty, lustful and sinful. Other people appear to be sincerely interested in sex but are impotent or frigid and thus unable to achieve a satisfactory sexual union. Sometimes this is because of the same fears and attitudes mentioned above, sometimes because of hostility toward the partner, and sometimes because the man and/or woman has never learned how to enjoy the sex act.

*Deviation in ways of sexual expression.* Exhibitionism, voyeurism, fetishism, transvestism, sadism and masochism are all terms which apply to abnormal ways of obtaining sexual satisfaction. Exhibitionism, which occurs almost exclusively in males and leads to one-third of all arrests for sexual offenses, involves the exposure in public of one's genitals. Voyeurism is "peeping tom" activity in which satisfaction comes from looking at sexually arousing situations. Fetishism involves the achievement of sexual satisfaction through the handling of some object, such as articles of clothing. Some men, for example, make a fetish of hair or of women's underclothes. When a person dresses and acts like a member of the opposite sex, the behavior is referred to as transvestism. Sadism and masochism are deviations in which the individual is sexually stimulated by inflicting pain on others (sadism) or on himself. Rape is often engaged in by sadists. The reasons for these various kinds of behavior are complex and often can be traced to the individual's upbringing and early experiences.

Masturbation, sexual pleasure through the manipulation of one's own genitals, is now recognized as being so common that it is often not even classified as deviant behavior. Although masturbation in no way harms one physically, it often brings considerable guilt and mental anguish, especially in adolescents. Many church leaders condemn it,

179

although it is not mentioned in the Bible.* Most psychologists and some Christians are of the opinion that this is a "necessary evil" that helps the person give expression to sexual urges before marriage. If masturbation persists after marriage or becomes a compulsion, this usually indicates immaturity, sexual fears, homosexual tendencies, or other underlying maladjustment.

*Deviation in choice of sex object.* Sexual contacts with a child, an animal, a variety of partners (promiscuity), a prostitute, a dead body, or a member of one's family (incest) are all considered deviant in our culture. While the church leader may occasionally encounter some of these forms of behavior, he (or she) is much more likely to come in contact with people who are sexually attracted to members of their own sex. This is homosexuality.

There are large individual differences in homosexual behavior. Some people are exclusively homosexual while others are sexually attracted to both sexes. Some are basically heterosexual but engage in homosexual acts when in prison, the military, boarding schools, or other situations when the opposite sex is not around. For some people, their attraction to same sex individuals is so well-hidden that it is not consciously recognized even by themselves. Others recognize that they have homosexual tendencies but are able to keep this a secret. Still others are overt homosexuals who freely engage in sexual relations with members of the same sex, "marry" their homosexual partners, and worship together in homosexual churches.

There are a number of misconceptions about homosexuality that should be discarded. For example, while many of these people are self-centered, immature, lonely and unhappy (not really "gay"), this does not mean that they are mentally ill. On the contrary, most homosexuals, like

*The sin of Onan (Gen. 38:8 ff.) is not masturbation. It is more often interpreted as *coitus interruptus* in which Onan disobeyed God by refusing to permit his dead brother's wife to bear children.

most heterosexuals, show no evidence of serious emotional disturbances.[20] Furthermore, homosexuals are not necessarily distinguishable by their physique or actions. While some male homosexuals are of slight build and effeminate in their mannerisms, many others are athletic, virile-looking men who give no hint of femininity. Also, there is no evidence to support the popular idea that homosexuals are especially creative. These people often engage in creative work, such as acting, hairdressing or interior decorating, but they are no more creative, productive or intelligent than nonhomosexuals.[21] Finally, it should not be assumed that homosexuality is organically caused. While there is still disagreement on this, most experts agree that homosexuality is an acquired condition wherein a person learns to fear and avoid the opposite sex, often because of his past experiences or upbringing. Of course the reasons for homosexuality are complex, and no one explanation can cover all cases.[22]

*Deviation in setting.* Some people can only be gratified sexually if they are in an illegal or otherwise forbidden situation, such as in a prostitute's room, in a car, or raping someone.

## CAUSES, TREATMENT AND PREVENTION OF DEVIATIONS

Sex deviates show a multitude of symptoms, their behavior may have any number of causes, and they can be treated with a variety of techniques. Studies of sexually maladjusted people frequently reveal one or more of the following: lack of opportunity to engage in normal sex behavior, isolation in childhood, unusual experiences in childhood or adolescence in which deviant sexuality is learned, fear of the opposite sex, fear of being hurt if one engages in normal sex, lack of opportunity to learn appropriate sex roles (e.g., in homes where there is no father, boys have difficulty learning how to act like a male), fear of adult responsibilities, sexual ignorance, and belief that normal sexual behavior is dirty or sinful.[23]

Many sexual deviations such as rape, molesting a child, exhibitionism, transvestism or sadistic acts are illegal and can result in an apprehended person being jailed. Regretfully, this incarceration does little, if anything, to eliminate the problem, and sometimes—with homosexuals, for example—the close contact with others in jail only accentuates the problem. Medical treatment also tends to be ineffective. Instead, it appears that psychotherapy and other kinds of psychological treatment are the most successful. But deviates often do not want to change. Their way of getting sexual satisfaction is pleasant and, in spite of social criticism, there is frequently a desire to persist in the deviation.

Once again, therefore, prevention is extremely important. Accurate sex education, preparation for healthy marital relationships, the alleviation of abnormal family situations, and guidance as the person grows to maturity, can all be important.[24] In each of these preventive measures, the church can play a role.

SEXUAL DEVIATION AND THE CHURCH

The author once counseled with a twenty-five-year-old married man who was a homosexual. He and his wife were both Christians who were active in the church. The man engaged in sexual relations with his wife, but he also (with his wife's knowledge) participated in overt sexual experiences with other men. When this became known to members of his church, he was voted out of the congregation, relieved of all responsibilities in the church, and informed, simply, that it would be acceptable for him to continue to attend services as long as he didn't get involved in any other church activities.

Society, in general, treats the sexually deviate person with great scorn, and many church people prefer to think that it is impossible to be a Christian *and* a sexual deviate. When deviation is discovered, there are shocked disbelief and immediate efforts to purge the congregation and community of such people. The deviate, in turn, comes to view himself as being dirty, "queer," unwanted, and something less than human. [25]

How should the Christian respond to sex deviates? One pastor made some suggestions in the following letter to the editor of *Christianity Today*:

> I am a homosexual and a minister of the Gospel. This may be shocking to many people, but it is not so shocking to Jesus Christ. He has been all sufficient, not only to forgive me, but also to give me control over this problem. Still I am a homosexual....
>
> Homosexuality is a manifestation of the lust of the flesh, never, in my opinion, of the love set forth in the Word of God....The homosexual often falls into a life of constant searching for sexual fulfillment; but he doesn't find it.... He moves from place to place, job to job. He is running, not only from society, but also from the lust within him. Finally he is discovered and condemned.
>
> What is the solution? Only the forgiveness of sin through Jesus Christ and constant deliverance through the Holy Spirit. The Word of God, in Romans 1:24-28, classifies homosexuality as sin—but by no means as the only or the gravest sin. It is listed among the sins of pride, boasting, gossiping, and others. Let us not condemn homosexuality any more— or less—than we would condemn the other sins of Romans 1.
>
> The temptation to homosexual activity endured by many Christians is like the "thorn in the flesh" that constantly bothered Paul. This temptation has drawn me closer to God than any other, and I can attest to the sufficiency of his Holy Spirit to give constant deliverance.
>
> I am a homosexual—but I am also a servant of the living Christ who experiences God's forgiveness and deliverance. By the grace of God this temptation does not express itself, and I am victorious through Christ. [26]

The Bible specifically condemns many of the sexual perversions. In the Old Testament law, the acts of incest, extramarital relations, homosexuality and sexual experiences with animals are all mentioned by name, described as sin, and specifically prohibited (Lev. 18:6-18, 20, 22-24, 30). The New Testament speaks against prostitution, fornication (premarital sex), adultery (extramarital sex) and homosexuality (Heb. 13:4; 1 Cor. 7:1-2; 1 Th. 4:2; Ro. 1:21-24). When the Bible talks of sex, it is referring to the union of a man and a woman who love each other and are "one flesh" in marriage (Heb. 13:4; Eph. 5:28-31; Mt. 19:5-6). To fit perversions into the biblical view of sex

> is impossible at every point. The sex act in marriage is the ultimate expression of love. The sex act performed apart from marriage falls short of this ultimate expression and leaves much to be desired. Often, if not always, it leaves both persons with a sense of guilt and lack of fulfillment. This is true of loveless marriages, of masturbation, and of homosexual activity. [27]

Faced with the reality of widespread sexual abuse and perversion, church leaders and other Christians have the following responsibilities:

*Acceptance of the sexually deviate.* The woman taken in adultery (Jn. 8) and the woman at the well (Jn. 4) had both been participating in sexually deviant behavior. Jesus did not approve of their sinful actions, but He did accept them as people in need.

It is easy to understand why parents would be reluctant to have a sexually maladjusted person teaching in the Sunday school or in an influential position of church leadership. But this does not mean that we should ostracize deviate people and kick them out of the church. We must accept them for what they are—individuals whom Christ loves, and people who need in a special way to experience the power and grace of God. Although He was criticized for doing so, Jesus spent time with publicans and sinners since these were the people whom He came to redeem. In like manner, we who are followers of Christ cannot cast off the sexual deviate as a hopeless untouchable.

*Counseling.* Sex deviates can profit from a frank discussion of their sexual problems, but counseling with these people is a very difficult task, especially if the counselor has little formal training or understanding of the problem. Exhorting the deviate to "change his ways" or to bury his problem under activities is usually ineffective,[28] and it may be more efficient to encourage the person to seek the help of a professional counselor.

*Education.* Church members should be taught both about deviations and about the biblical standards for mature sexual expression. An understanding of these facts is important if we are to prevent deviation and help those who are having sexual problems.

## CRIME AND DELINQUENCY

We are living in an age when crime appears to be on the march. Violence in the streets, rioting, civil disobedience, juvenile delinquency—all are on the increase. And despite the concern of numerous public officials, things are not getting any better; they're getting worse.

The middle-class church member might prefer to ignore this crime explosion, to shake his head in amazement at the headlines, to keep his doors locked, and to hope that somehow he will be protected from the actions of violent men. But this ostrich-type behavior is never condoned in Scripture. Even Jesus was concerned about crime, and He successfully counseled at least one man who appears to have been a "white-collar" thief (Lk. 19:1-9).

For the purpose of discussion, let us divide those who engage in illegal acts into four groups:

### ANTISOCIAL PERSONALITIES

The category of antisocial personalities includes swindlers, forgers, liars, imposters, unprincipled businessmen, "crooked" politicians and similar social misfits. Such people (who are sometimes called sociopaths) are often charming, well-liked and intelligent, but they are also impulsive,

185

irresponsible, and without moral or ethical standards. Most of their behavior is geared to the present, so if lying, cheating, stealing, or even apologizing seems appropriate, the antisocial person will act in this way, giving no thought to the consequences. His philosophy seems to be, "Do what you want today and never worry about tomorrow." When such a person does get into trouble with the authorities, he may express remorse but he has no sense of guilt and rarely does he learn from his punishment.

Although antisocial behavior may have some biological causes, it seems likely that the home background is of greater importance. The antisocial person may have learned from his parents how to "put on a front," but he has never learned standards of right and wrong which he really accepts. If he comes for counseling, this type of person may cooperate with a counselor and say the right things in an interview, but there is little desire to change. More often such people spontaneously decide to alter their behavior as they get older.

### DYSSOCIAL INDIVIDUALS

In growing up, most children acquire standards of behavior from those around them. If the child comes from a family of criminals or if his siblings and peers are delinquents, he will acquire the values of these groups. Dyssocial people are not emotionally disturbed. They often have intense loyalties and well-defined standards of behavior, but these loyalties are to other criminals; the standards which they accept are rejected by the mainstream of the culture. Jail keeps such people from society, but it does little or nothing to change their well-developed criminal tendencies.

### OTHER ADULT DELINQUENTS

There is evidence to suggest that most adult crimes are committed by people who would be classified as antisocial or dyssocial. A few juvenile delinquents carry their behavior into adulthood and, in addition, perhaps one-third of the crimes for which people are prosecuted are carried out by drug addicts, alcoholics, sex deviates, neurotics, and mildly disturbed psychotics.[29]

Within recent years, however, we have seen increasing evidence for another type of adult crime. It is more impulsive and sometimes comes because of social pressure, a desire for "kicks," a wish to "look sharp" in front of one's friends, or a belief that violence is the most efficient way to get what one wants. Racial riots, student rebellion and vandalism are included in this category.

Recently the newspapers reported a robbery committed by a lone, well-dressed woman in her early twenties. This young person was a college student who was driving home after visiting friends in the East. Since she was running short of money, she impulsively decided to hold up a little drugstore. She had never done this before, had no criminal record, and came from a well-to-do home, but she had seen robberies on television and decided to try for herself. After fleeing with her loot, she suddenly recognized the implications of her act and returned to the drugstore just as the police were arriving.

Many people today are concluding that violence and crime *do* pay. The successful experiences of others (portrayed so vividly in the mass media), the belief that "I probably won't get caught," and the knowledge that fines and prison sentences today are relatively light, apparently combine to stimulate acts of illegal behavior in people who are otherwise law-abiding citizens. How we prevent this kind of civil disobedience is a problem which is being discussed and studied by many people.[30] The answers are not likely to be simple.

## JUVENILE DELINQUENTS

In the United States alone, well over a million young people under the age of eighteen get into serious trouble with the law every year. So prevalent is delinquency that literally thousands of research studies have focused on the

187

problem. These studies have shown that most delinquents tend to have unfavorable attitudes toward school, confused moral values, idle time, unfavorable home conditions (including broken homes, rejection by the father, overdomination by the mother, parental absenteeism), poor neighborhoods (including overcrowding, impoverished conditions, and the presence of delinquent gangs), feelings of inadequacy and hostility, "athletic" body build, and below-average intelligence.[31] In addition, delinquents rarely have much religious training. According to the late J. Edgar Hoover, "In practically every home where juvenile delinquency is bred, there is an absence of religious training in children. . . . Most of them have never been inside a church."[32] At home these young people have seen low parental standards of right and wrong and have had little clear moral training. When children grow up with too little restraint and too little sense of moral obligation, writes the famous Dr. Spock, they "are likely to be miserable in childhood, to get into trouble in adolescence and to be unhappy and ineffectual in adulthood."[33]

Such a listing of some *characteristics* of delinquents doesn't tell us much about the *causes* of delinquency. There are many delinquents who have different backgrounds than that described above, and thousands of other young people who never engage in delinquent behavior but come from broken homes or deteriorating neighborhoods. We are left then with the frustrating conclusion that there are no simple causes—or simple solutions—to the problem of juvenile delinquency.

To understand and help these young people, there must be a pooling of community resources, including the police, juvenile court officials, youth club personnel, schoolteachers and administrators, parents, and church members. There must be an attempt to improve the social and family conditions which are most likely to breed delinquency, and there must be community efforts to provide recreational and counseling facilities.

In addition to cooperating with community groups, the church leader can make two significant contributions. First, he can provide the moral guidance that delinquent teenagers and their parents so often need. The Word of God does not speak on every specific ethical issue, but it does contain broad moral guidelines for the modern world. Second, we must never underestimate the power of God for changing men's lives. Before His death, Christ's last convert was a thief. In more modern times, we have seen the transformation of criminals like Jim Vaas and juvenile gang leaders like Tom Skinner.[34] The average delinquent never darkens the door of a church, but he may often come into contact with church leaders.* On such occasions we must be warm and concerned, rather than coldly authoritarian,[35] and we must not be afraid to introduce the Christ who can lift young people and old and set their feet on a rock (Ps. 40:1-4).

## IS DEVIANT BEHAVIOR A SICKNESS OR A SIN?

Preaching in itself is an ineffective way to treat and prevent the various syndromes which have been described in this chapter. The Salvation Army has long realized the need to combine the gospel with a bed and opportunities for rehabilitation; foreign missionaries teach school or work in hospitals in addition to their preaching; and hopefully, most contemporary church leaders realize that they must do more than say, "Depart in peace, be ye warmed and filled" (Ja. 2:16) and then offer no practical help.

The help that we give will depend somewhat on our views of whether socially deviate behavior is sinful or a symptom of some underlying sickness. If the deviate is considered

---

*For a very dramatic portrayal of a pastor who is also a police officer working with juvenile gangs see *On Patrol for God*, a 30-minute motion picture available from CURE, 3644 N. Broad Street, Philadelphia, Pa., 19140.

to be a responsible individual who willingly engages in antisocial behavior, then he must be expected to pay for his
crime by going to prison or by paying a fine. Accordingly,
the old McNaughten rule, which was established in 1843
and still prevails in most English-speaking countries,

> to establish a defense on the ground of insanity, it must be
> clearly proved, that at the time of committing the act, the
> party accused was laboring under such a defect of reason
> from disease of the mind, as not to know the nature and
> quality of the act he was doing, or if he did know it, that he
> did not know he was doing what was wrong.

According to this view, antisocial behavior is wrong (i.e.,
sinful) and even emotionally disturbed people must pay for
their crimes if they knew at the time that their actions were
wrong. In contrast, the Durham Rule, which was handed
down in 1954 in the District of Columbia, states that "an
accused is not criminally responsible if his unlawful act was
the product of mental disease or defect." Even if the person
knew that his act was wrong, this view holds, he is not responsible if he was mentally ill at the time.[36] Such persons
are not imprisoned but are sent instead to a mental hospital or even released from custody. Recent findings that some
criminals have genetic abnormalities have given further
support to this viewpoint.[37]

The "sin-or-sickness controversy" is of interest to more
people than judges or lawyers. Many fear that large numbers
of known criminals are being let off scot-free because they
claim to have been insane at the time of their crimes. In
considering his own stand on this issue, the churchman
must deal with the following facts:

*All social deviates are not sick, but all are maladjusted
in some way and thus in need of treatment.*

*Psychology and psychiatry do not really know how to treat
and rehabilitate deviant individuals.* A good start has been
made in this direction, but the problems are so complex

and the available personnel so few that rehabilitation efforts are still relatively unsuccessful.

*Prisons don't work very well.* Because of inadequate staff and overcrowding, prisoners simply "serve time." If they learn anything, it is how to be a better criminal when they get out.[38]

*We must be concerned both about deviate persons and about the general public.* Our concern for criminals must be coupled with a realization that law-abiding citizens also have rights and must be protected.

*It is impossible to determine at a later time if a person was "insane" when he committed a crime.* The inability to agree on this is demonstrated whenever psychologists and psychiatrists testify in a court of law.

*The Bible holds men responsible for sin and gives no indication that men who are psychotic or ignorant are "without excuse"* (Ro. 1:18-2:16).

The church leader and every other Christian are responsible for reaching men with the good news that, even though all are sinners, God forgives (Ro. 3:23; 1 Jn. 1:9), and transforms the lives of those who put their trust in Christ (2 Cor. 5:17; Ro. 12:2). To spread this message, to help young people find new life in Christ, and to guide in their day-to-day behavior may seem like a small part to play in the prevention and treatment of delinquency, but it has implications both for the present and for eternity.

## SUMMARY

Whereas some people react to the stresses of life by withdrawing into psychotic or neurotic states, others express their frustrations more openly in acts that are antisocial. Alcoholics and drug addicts first get high on relatively small quantities of alcohol or drugs, and then the user becomes addicted. The sexual deviates and the delinquents satisfy their personal needs and desires in ways which are usually inconsiderate of others and against the norms of the society. Unless he is completely withdrawn into an ecclesiastical

191

ivory tower, the church leader will often encounter these socially deviate people. He must respond with understanding, practical help, and a willingness to share the good news that God loves, forgives, and transforms lives.

## NOTES

### Preface
1. O. H. Mowrer, "What Is Normal Behavior?" in *Introduction to Clinical Psychology*, ed. E. A. Berg and L. A. Pennington, pp. 58-88.
2. Ruth Benedict, *Patterns of Culture.*

### Chapter 1
1. P. Naitoh, *Sleep Loss and Its Effect on Performance.*
2. E. Rosen and I. Gregory, *Abnormal Psychology*, pp. 110-11.
3. A. Keys et al., *The Biology of Human Starvation.*
4. I. L. Janis, *Psychological Stress.*
5. O. W. Kisker, *The Disorganized Personality.*
6. K. Goldstein, *The Organism.*
7. Rosen and Gregory.
8. L. H. Long, ed., *The World Almanac and Book of Facts* (1970 edition). New York: Doubleday, 1969.
9. S. Glueck and E. Glueck, *Predicting Delinquency and Crime.*
10. J. W. Gardner, *Self-Renewal: The Individual and the Innovative Society*, p. 6.
11. A. Toffler, *Future Shock.*
12. M. Sherman and T. R. Henry, *Hollow Folk.*
13. G. R. Collins, *A Psychologist Looks at Life.*
14. O. H. Mowrer, *The Crisis in Psychiatry and Religion.*
15. H. B. English and Ava C. English, *A Comprehensive Dictionary of Psychological and Psychoanalytical Terms*, p. 234.
16. Kisker.
17. Mowrer, pp. 167, 217.
18. W. Lord, *A Night to Remember.*
19. D. Rosenthal, *Genetics of Psychopathology.*
20. Rosen and Gregory.
21. T. S. Langner and S. T. Michael, *Life Stress and Mental Health.*
22. J. C. Coleman and W. Broen, *Abnormal Psychology and Modern Life.*
23. P. H. Mussen, J. J. Conger and J. Kagan, *Child Development and Personality.*
14. L. P. Thrope, B. Katz and R. T. Lewis, *The Psychology of Abnormal Behavior*, p. 68.
25. A. B. Hollingshead and F. C. Redlich, *Social Class and Mental Illness: A Community Study.*
26. A. Davis and R. J. Havighurst, "Social Class and Color Differences in Child Rearing," *American Sociological Review* 11 (1946): 698-710.
27. L. Strole et al., *Mental Health in the Metropolis: The Midtown Manhattan Study.* Vol. 1.

28. J. W. Eaton and R. J. Weil, "The Mental Health of the Hutterites," *Scientific American* 189 (1953): 31-37.
29. W. H. Grier and P. M. Cobbs, *Black Rage*.
30. H. C. Cayton, "The Psychology of the Negro Under Discrimination" in *Mental Health and Mental Disorder: A Sociological Approach*, pp. 380-81.
31. G. Gurin, J. Veroff and S. Feld, *Americans View Their Mental Health: A Nationwide Survey*.
32. Joint Commission on Mental Illness and Health, *Action for Mental Health: Final Report of the Joint Commission on Mental Illness and Health*.
33. Edith Weisskopf-Joelson, "Logotherapy and Existential Analysis," *Acta Psychotherapeutica* 6 (1958): 193-304.
34. B. Russell, *Why I Am Not A Christian: And Other Essays on Religion and Related Subjects*.
35. L. Granberg, "Psychiatry and Christianity: Beyond Theory," *His* 24 (June 1964): 14.
36. A. W. Combs and D. Snygg, *Individual Behavior: A Perceptual Approach to Behavior*.

## Chapter 2

1. M. Zax and G. Stricker, *Patterns of Psychopathology: Case Studies of Behavioral Dysfunction*, pp. 69-72.
2. W. E. Oates, *When Religion Gets Sick*.
3. Zax and Stricker, p. 69.
4. S. Freud, *Civilization and Its Discontents*.
5. E. Fromm, *The Sane Society*, p. 15.
6. J. A. Knight, "The Use and Misuse of Religion by the Emotional Disturbed," *Pastoral Psychology* 13 (1962): 10-18; Oates; and A. Trew, "The Religious Factor in Mental Illness," *Pastoral Psychology* 22 (May 1971): 21-28.
7. V. E. Frankl, *Man's Search for Meaning*.
8. E. Sauer, *In the Arena of Faith*, p. 54.
9. American Psychiatric Assn., Committee on Nomenclature and Statistics, *Diagnostic and Statistical Manual of Mental Disorders*.

## Chapter 3

1. G. Gurin, J. Veroff and S. Feld, *Americans View Their Mental Health: A Nationwide Survey*.
2. Joint Commission on Mental Illness and Health, *Action for Mental Health: Final Report of the Joint Commission on Mental Illness and Health*.
3. J. D. Matarazzo, "The Interview," in *Handbook of Clinical Psychology*, ed. B. B. Wolman, p. 403.
4. Ibid.
5. "Technical Recommendations for Psychological Tests and Diagnostic Techniques," *Psychological Bulletin* 51 (1954).
6. R. L. Mooney, *Mooney Problem Check List*.
7. G. W. Kisker, *The Disorganized Personality*, p. 483.
8. Frances K. Graham and Barbara S. Kendall, "Memory-for-Designs Test," *Perceptual and Motor Skills* 11 (1960): 147-88.
9. E. E. Bruder, *Ministering to Deeply Troubled People*; L. H. DeWolf, "Needed: All-Round Pastoral Training," *Pastoral Psychology* 20 (Mar. 1969): 7-9; and E. M. Pattison,"Functions of the Clergy in Community Mental Health Centers," *Pastoral Psychology* 16 (1965): 21-26.
10. E. Peterson, *Psychopharmacology*.

193

11. J. C. Coleman and W. Broen, *Abnormal Psychology and Modern Life*.
12. J. C. Watkins, "Psychotherapeutic Methods" in *Handbook of Clinical Psychology*, ed. B. B. Wolman, pp. 1143-67.
13. A. Lazarus, *Behavior Therapy and Beyond*.
14. V. E. Frankl, *Man's Search for Meaning*.
15. P. Bindrim, "Nudity as a Quick Grab for Intimacy in Group Therapy," *Psychology Today* (June 1969): 24-28; and E. E. Mintz, *Marathon Groups: Reality and Symbol*.
16. D. F. Tweedie, *The Christian and the Couch: An Introduction to Christian Logotherapy*, p. 33.
17. O. H. Mowrer, *The Crisis in Psychiatry and Religion*.
18. Edith Weisskopf-Joelson, "Logotherapy and Existential Analysis," *Acta Psychotherapeutica* 6 (1958): 193-304.
19. J. Greenspoon, "Verbal Conditioning and Clinical Psychology" in *Experimental Foundations of Clinical Psychology*, ed. A. J. Bachrach; and Matarazzo.
20. C. M. Lowe, "Value Orientations—An Ethical Dilemma," *American Psychologist* 14 (1959): 687-93.
21. E. T. Gendlin and J. F. Rychlak, "Psychotherapeutic Processes," *Annual Review of Psychology* 21 (1970): 155-90.
22. H. J. Eysenck, "The Effects of Psychotherapy" in *Handbook of Abnormal Psychology: An Experimental Approach*, ed. H. J. Eysenck, pp. 697-725.
23. W. Clopton, "Is Psychotherapy Tool or Fraud?" *St. Paul Sunday Pioneer Press* (Oct. 10, 1965).

### Chapter 4

1. E. Bleuler, *Dementia Praecox, or the Group of Schizophrenias*.
2. J. C. Coleman, *Abnormal Psychology and Modern Life*, p. 277.
3. R. M. Goldenson, *The Encyclopedia of Human Behavior: Psychology, Psychiatry, and Mental Health*, p. 1160.
4. B. B. Wolman, "Schizophrenia and Related Disorders" in *Handbook of Clinical Psychology*, ed. B. B. Wolman, p. 1013.
5. Coleman.
6. G. W. Kisker, *The Disorganized Personality*, p. 375.
7. E. Rosen and I. Gregory, *Abnormal Psychology*, p. 227.
8. S. B. Kutash, "Psychoneuroses" in *Handbook of Clinical Psychology*, pp. 948-75.
9. Coleman, p. 194.
10. Adapted from B. A. Maher, *Principles of Psychopathology: An Experimental Approach*, p. 174.
11. L. D. Weatherhead, *Psychology, Religion and Healing*, p. 158.
12. J. D. Frank, *Persuasion and Healing: A Comparative Study of Psychotherapy*, p. 58.
13. W. Bonime, "Dynamics and Psychotherapy of Depression" in *Current Psychiatric Therapies*, ed. J. H. Masserman, 2:137-46.
14. G. C. Bonnell, "The Pastor's Role in Counseling the Depressed," *Pastoral Psychology* 21 (Jan. 1970): 38-46; and P. W. Pretzel, "The Role of the Clergyman in Suicide Prevention," *Pastoral Psychology* 21 (Apr. 1970): 47-52.
15. Kisker, p. 229.
16. Ibid., p. 227.
17. L. P. Thrope, B. Katz and R. T. Lewis, *The Psychology of Abnormal Behavior*.
18. J. C. Coleman and W. Broen, *Abnormal Psychology and Modern Life*.

19. P. Friedman and L. Linn, "Some Psychiatric Notes on the *Andrea Doria* Disaster," *American Journal of Psychiatry* 114 (1957): 426-32.
20. Kisker, p. 204.
21. P. Solomon et al., *Sensory Deprivation*; and C. Leuba, "Toward Some Integration of Learning Theories: The Concept of Optimal Stimulation," *Psychological Reports* 1 (1955): 27-33.
22. W. H. Bexton, W. Heron and T. H. Scott, "Effects of Decreased Variation in the Sensory Environment," *Canadian Journal of Psychology* 8 (1954): 70-76.
23. W. Sargant, *Battle for the Mind: A Physiology of Conversion and Brain Washing*, p. 150.
24. Coleman and Broen.
25. H. Stierlin, "Psychoses" in *The Encyclopedia of Mental Health*, 5:1664.

## Chapter 5

1. E. C. Hoff, "Alcoholism" in *The Encyclopedia of Mental Health*, 1:179.
2. H. J. Clinebell, Jr., *Understanding and Counseling the Alcoholic*.
3. D. Lum, "The Church and the Prevention of Alcoholism," *Journal of Religion and Health* 9 (Apr. 1970): 138-61.
4. Clinebell, "The Agony of the Family of the Alcoholic," *Pastoral Psychology* 13 (Apr. 1962): 5-7, 65; and J. K. Jackson, "Alcoholism as a Family Crisis," *Pastoral Psychology* 13 (Apr. 1962): 8-18.
5. Cooperative Commission on the Study of Alcoholism, *Alcohol Problems: A Report to the Nation*.
6. Clinebell, *Understanding and Counseling the Alcoholic*.
7. T. L. Duncan, *Understanding and Helping the Narcotic Addict*.
8. R. Marcucci, "The Medical Aspects of Drug Abuse" and J. Dobson, *Dare to Discipline*.
9. D. P. Ausubel, *Drug Addiction: Physiological, Psychological, and Sociological Aspects*; and A. Bassin, "Daytop Village," *Psychology Today* 2 (Dec. 2, 1968): 48-52, 68.
10. Ausubel, "An Evaluation of Recent Adolescent Drug Addiction," *Mental Hygiene* 36 (1952): 373-82.
11. Duncan, p. 29.
12. Bassin.
13. L. Yablonsky, *Synanon: The Tunnel Back*; and Bassin.
14. D. Wilkerson, *The Cross and the Switchblade*.
15. G. J. Jennings, "Drug Use and American Culture" in *Our Society in Turmoil*, ed. G. R. Collins, pp. 81-97.
16. D. N. Lombardi, "The Special Language of the Addict," *Pastoral Psychology* 20 (June 1969): 51-52.
17. W. Simon, "Sex," *Psychology Today* 3 (July 1968): 23.
18. J. C. Coleman and W. Broen, *Abnormal Psychology and Modern Life*.
19. A. C. Kinsey, W. B. Pomeroy and C. E. Martin, "Concepts of Normality and Abnormality in Sexual Behavior" in *Psychosexual Development in Health and Disease*, p. 28.
20. M. Hoffman, "Homosexual," *Psychology Today* 3 (July 1969): 43-45, 70.
21. W. Bromberg, "Homosexuality" in *The Encyclopedia of Mental Health*, 3: 747-64.
22. D. J. West, *Homosexuality*; and D. L. Farnsworth, "Sexual Aberrations," *Journal of Religion and Health* 7 (Oct. 1968): 350-57.
23. E. Rosen and I. Gregory, *Abnormal Psychology*.

24. J. C. Coleman and W. Broen, *Abnormal Psychology and Modern Life*.
25. Hoffman.
26. Anonymous, "Letter from a Homosexual," *Christianity Today* 12 (Mar. 1, 1968): 547.
27. Ibid.
28. H. K. Jones, *Toward a Christian Understanding of the Homosexual*.
29. Coleman and Broen.
30. See Dobson.
31. Coleman and Broen; S. Glueck and E. Glueck, *Predicting Delinquency and Crime*; Elizabeth Hurlock, *Adolescent Development*; and A. J. Kahn, "Juvenile Delinquency" in *The Encyclopedia of Mental Health*, pp. 893-907.
32. As quoted by Hurlock, pp. 479-80.
33. B. Spock, "Psychology Can't Substitute for Morality" in *Morality and Mental Health*, ed. O. H. Mowrer, p. 42.
34. Tom Skinner, *Black and Free*. Grand Rapids: Zondervan, 1968.
35. W. E. Alberts, "Minister's Attitudes Toward Delinquency," *Pastoral Psychology* 18 (Sept. 1967): 7-14.
36. B. L. Diamond, "Law and Psychiatry" in *The Encyclopedia of Mental Health*, ed. A. Deutsch and H. Fishmann, 3:908-29; and S. Glueck, "Mental Illness and Criminal Responsibility," *Pastoral Psychology* 18 (Feb. 1967): 31-47.
37. A. Montagu, "Chromosomes and Crime," *Psychology Today*, 2 (October, 1968): 43-49.
38. K. Menninger, M. Mayman and P. Pruyser, *The Vital Balance*.

# SUGGESTIONS FOR FURTHER READING

## Chapter 1

The causes of abnormal behavior are discussed in most basic textbooks of psychiatry and abnormal psychology. Of these, the following are well written and contain good treatments of the topic: E. Rosen and I. Gregory, *Abnormal Psychology*, G. W. Kisker, *The Disorganized Personality*, and J. C. Coleman and W. Broen, *Abnormal Psychology and Modern Life*. O. H. Mowrer's position is summarized in his *The Crisis in Psychiatry and Religion\** and *Morality and Mental Health*. Both would be of special interest to church leaders. For a fascinating summary of V. E. Frankl's position, see his little book *Man's Search for Meaning.\** M. H. Nelson's *Why Christians Crack Up* is overly simplified, but discusses some of the issues relating to abnormal behavior in Christians.

## Chapter 2

The subject matter in this chapter is discussed in most textbooks of abnormal psychology. Among the most widely used of these are books by J. C. Coleman and W. Broen, *Abnormal Psychology and Modern Life*, G. G. Kisker, *The Disorganized Personality*, and E. Rosen and I. Gregory, *Abnormal Psychology*.

*The Diagnostic and Statistical Manual of Mental Disorders,\** published by the American Psychiatric Association, is the source from which Table 2-2 is summarized. A discussion of the historical background and modern problems in classification is found in an article by Brill, "Psychiatric Diagnosis, Nomenclature, and Classification." (1965). Karl Menninger, et al., *The Vital Balance*, gives the unique classification scheme of the author, who is probably America's most famous psychiatrist.

For discussions of mental illness and religion, see W. E. Oates, *When Religion Gets Sick\** and G. H. Anderson, *Your Religion: Neurotic or Healthy?*

## Chapter 3

An inexpensive little book by L. E. Tyler, *Tests and Measurements,\** gives a brief introduction to psychological testing. More detailed accounts of assessment are given in L. J. Cronback, *Essentials of Psychological Testing*, H. H. Anderson and G. L. Anderson, *An Introduction to Projective Testing*, and L. Goldman, *Using Tests in Counseling*.

*Modern Clinical Psychiatry*, by A. P. Noyes and L. C. Kolb, has gone through numerous revisions, but is a basic textbook dealing with both assessment and treatment. R. A. Harper, *Psychoanalysis and Psychother-*

197

*apy*,* gives a brief introduction to thirty-six different approaches to treatment. For a more extensive introduction, see Patterson, *Theories of Counseling and Psychotherapy*. In addition, there is a discussion of treatment in each of the textbooks listed under chapter 1. J. H. Masserman's *Modern Therapy of Personality Disorders** is readable and inexpensive. Finally, E. E. Bruder's *Ministering to Deeply Troubled People** is written specifically for pastors. The techniques of counseling are discussed more fully in the second volume of this series, *Restoration: The Psychology of Counseling.*

## Chapter 4

Any book in abnormal psychology or basic psychiatry will give more detailed discussion of the syndromes that are discussed in this chapter. In preparing this chapter, the author leaned heavily on J. C. Coleman and W. Broen's *Abnormal Psychology and Modern Life*, G. G. Kisker's *The Disorganized Personality*, E. Rosen and I. Gregory's *Abnormal Psychology*, and a technical book edited by B. B. Wolman, *Handbook of Clinical Psychology*. Less technical and shorter treatments of the subject are given by J. R. Strange in *Abnormal Psychology* and W. J. Corille, et al , *Abnormal Psychology.** The subject of suicide is discussed briefly in articles by M. O. Vincent in *Christianity Today* and by P. W. Pretzel in *Pastoral Psychology.*

For the reader who wants to read some "first-person accounts" of what abnormality is like, see B. Kaplan, *The Inner World of Mental Illness.** An excellent series of case histories is included in M. Zax and G. Stricker's *The Study of Abnormal Behavior: Selected Readings.** See also, E. B. McNeil, *The Quiet Furies.**

## Chapter 5

Four volumes in the Successful Pastoral Counseling Series are directly related to the subject matter of this chapter: H. H. Cassler, *Ministering to Prisoners and Their Families,** T. L. Duncan, *Understanding and Helping the Narcotic Addict,** F. I. Frellick, *Helping Youth in Conflict,** and T. J. Shipp, *Helping the Alcoholic and His Family.*

H. J. Clinebell's *Understanding and Counseling the Alcoholic* is the best treatment on alcoholism that the minister will find. Although not written for church leaders, D. P. Ausubel's *Drug Addiction: Physiological, Psychological, and Sociological Aspects** is one of several concise treatments of this topic. F. Ridenour, *It All Depends** and S. B. Babbage, *Christianity and Sex** are written for young people and deal with the new morality and sex. The church leader may also find helpful information in H. K. Jones, *Toward a Christian Understanding of the Homosexual.*

*Available in paperback editions.

# BIBLIOGRAPHY

Alberts, W. E. "Minister's Attitudes Toward Delinquency," *Pastoral Psychology* 18 (Sept. 1967): 7-14.

American Social Health Assn. *A Guide to Some Drugs Which Are Subject to Abuse.* New York: ASHA, 1968.

American Psychiatric Assn. Committee on Nomenclature and Statistics. *Diagnostic and Statistical Manual of Mental Disorders.* 2nd ed. Washington, D. C., 1968.

Anonymous, "Letter from a Homosexual," *Christianity Today* 12 (Mar. 1, 1968): 547.

Anderson, G. H. *Your Religion: Neurotic or Healthy?* Garden City, N. Y.: Doubleday, 1970.

Anderson, H. H. and Anderson, G. L., eds. *An Introduction to Projective Techniques.* Englewood Cliffs, N. J.: Prentice-Hall, 1951.

Ausubel, D. P. *Drug Addiction: Physiological, Psychological, and Sociological Aspects.* New York: Random House, 1958.

– – –. "An Evaluation of Recent Adolescent Drug Addiction," *Mental Hygiene* 36 (1952): 373-82.

– – –. *Theory and Problems of Adolescent Development.* New York: Grune & Stratton, 1954.

Babbage, S. B. *Christianity and Sex.* Chicago: Inter-Varsity, 1963.

Bassin, A. "Daytop Village," *Psychology Today* 2 (Dec. 2, 1968): 48-52, 68.

Benedict, Ruth, *Patterns of Culture.* New York: Mentor Books, 1934.

Bexton, G. H.; Heron, W. and Scott, T. H. "Effects of Decreased Variation in the Sensory Environment," *Canadian Journal of Psychology* 8 (1954): 70-76.

Bindrim, P. "Nudity as a Quick Grab for Intimacy in Group Therapy," *Psychology Today* 3 (June 1969): 24-28.

Bleuler, E. *Dementia Praecox, or the Group of Schizophrenias.* New York: International Universities Press, 1952.

Bonime, W. "Dynamics and Psychotherapy of Depression" in *Current Psychiatric Therapies*, ed. J. H. Masserman. Vol. 2. New York: Grune & Stratton, 1962, pp. 137-46.

Bonnell, G. C. "The Pastor's Role in Counseling the Depressed," *Pastoral Psychology* 21 (Jan. 1970): 38-46.

Brayfield, A. H. "Psychology as a Profession," *American Psychologist* 23 (1968): 195-200.

Bromberg, W. "Homosexuality" in *The Encyclopedia of Mental Health*, ed. A. Deutsch and H. Fishman. Vol. 3. New York: Watts, 1963, pp. 747-64.

Bruder, E. E. *Ministering to Deeply Troubled People*. Philadelphia: Fortress, 1964.

— — —. "The Pastoral Ministry to the Mentally Ill," *Pastoral Psychology* 17 (1966): 23-27.

Cassler, H. H. *Ministering to Prisoners and Their Families*. Philadelphia: Fortress, 1969.

Cayton, H. C. "The Psychology of the Negro Under Discrimination" in *Mental Health and Mental Disorder: A Sociological Approach*, ed. A. M. Rose. New York: Norton, 1955, pp. 377-92.

Clark, W. H. *Chemical Ecstacy: Psychedelic Drugs and Religion*. New York: Sheed & Ward, 1969.

Clopton, W. "Is Psychotherapy Tool or Fraud?" *St. Paul Sunday Pioneer Press*. (St. Paul, Minn.) (Oct. 10, 1965).

Clinebell, H. J., Jr. "The Agony of the Family of the Alcoholic," *Pastoral Psychology* 13 (Apr. 1962): 5-7, 65.

— — —. *Understanding and Counseling the Alcoholic*. Rev. Ed. New York: Abingdon, 1968.

Coleman, J. C. *Abnormal Psychology and Modern Life*. 3d ed. Chicago: Scott-Foresman, 1964.

Coleman, J. C. and Broen, W. *Abnormal Psychology and Modern Life*. 4th ed. Glenview, Ill.: Scott-Foresman, 1972.

Collins, G. R. *A Psychologist Looks at Life*. Wheaton, Ill.: Key, 1971.

Combs, A. W. and Snygg, D. *Individual Behavior: A Perceptual Approach to Behavior*. Rev. ed. New York: Harper, 1959.

Cooperative Commission on the Study of Alcoholism. *Alcohol Problems: A Report to the Nation*. New York: Oxford U., 1967.

Coville, W. J.; Costello, T. W. and Rouke, F. L. *Abnormal Psychology: Mental Illness Types, Causes, and Treatments*. New York: Barnes & Noble, 1960.

Cronbach, L. J. *Essentials of Psychological Testing*. 2d ed. New York: Harper, 1960.

Davis, A. and Havighurst, R. J. "Social Class and Color Differences in Child Rearing," *American Sociological Review* 11 (1946): 698-710.

"Death and Suspense on an Alpine Cable," *Life* 61, no. 4 (July 22, 1966): 29.

DeWolf, L. H. "Needed: All-Round Pastoral Training," *Pastoral Psychology* 20 (Mar. 1969): 7-9.

Diamond, B. L. "Law and Psychiatry" in *The Encyclopedia of Mental Health*, ed. A. Deutsch and H. Fishman. Vol. 3. New York: Watts, 1963, pp 908-29.

Dobson, J. *Dare to Discipline*. Wheaton, Ill.: Tyndale, 1970.

Duncan, T. L. *Understanding and Helping the Narcotic Addict.* Philadelphia: Fortress, 1968.

Eaton, J. W. and Weil, R. J. "The Mental Health of the Hutterites," *Scientific American* 189 (1953): 31-37.

English, H. B. and English, Ava C. *A Comprehensive Dictionary of Psychological and Psychoanalytical Terms.* New York: Longmans, Green, 1958.

Eysenck, H. J. "The Effects of Psychotherapy" in *Handbook of Abnormal Psychology: An Experimental Approach*, ed. H. J. Eysenck. New York: Basic Books, 1961, pp. 697-725.

Farberow, N. L. and Shneidman, E. S. *The Cry for Help.* New York: McGraw-Hill, 1961.

Farnsworth, D. L. "Sexual Aberrations," *Journal of Religion and Health* 7 (Oct. 1968): 350-57.

Frank, J. D. *Persuasion and Healing: A Comparative Study of Psychotherapy.* New York: Schocken Books, 1961.

Frankl, V. E. *Man's Search for Meaning.* New York: Washington Square, 1959.

Frellick, F. I. *Helping Youth in Conflict.* Philadelphia: Fortress, 1968.

Freud, S. *Civilization and Its Discontents.* London: Hogarth, 1953.

Friedman, P. and Linn, L. "Some Psychiatric Notes on the *Andrea Doria* Disaster," *American Journal of Psychiatry* 114 (1957): 426-32.

Fromm, E. *The Sane Society.* New York: Rhinehart, 1955.

Gardner, J. W. *Self-Renewal: The Individual and the Innovative Society.* New York: Harper & Row, 1963.

Gendlin, E. T. and Rychlak, J. F. "Psychotherapeutic Processes," *Annual Review of Psychology* 21 (1970): 155-90.

Glasser, William. *Mental Health or Mental Illness?* New York: Harper & Row, 1970.

Glatt, M. M. "Group Therapy in Alcoholism," *British Journal of Addiction* 54 (1957).

Glueck, S. "Mental Illness and Criminal Responsibility," *Pastoral Psychology* 18 (Feb. 1967): 31-47.

Glueck, S. and Glueck, E. *Predicting Delinquency and Crime.* Cambridge: Harvard U., 1959.

Gluckman, R. M. "The Chaplain as a Member of the Diagnostic Clinical Team," *Mental Hygiene* 37 (1953): 278-82.

Goldenson, R. M. *The Encyclopedia of Human Behavior: Psychology, Psychiatry, and Mental Health.* Garden City, N. Y.: Doubleday, 1970.

Goldman, L. *Using Tests in Counseling.* New York: Appleton-Century-Crofts, 1971.

Goldstein, K. *The Organism.* New York: American Book, 1939.

Graham, Frances K. and Kendall, Barbara S. "Memory-for-Designs Test (rev. general manual)," *Perceptual and Motor Skills* 11 (1960): 147-88.

Granberg, L. "Psychiatry and Christianity: Beyond Theory," *His* 24 (June 1964): 11-16.

Greenspoon, J. "Verbal Conditioning and Clinical Psychology" in *Experimental Foundations of Clinical Psychology*, ed. A. J. Bachrach. New York: Basic Books, 1962, pp. 510-53.

Grier, W. H. and Cobbs, P. M. *Black Rage*. New York: Basic Books, 1968.

Gurin, G.; Veroff, J. and Feld, S. *Americans View Their Mental Health: A Nationwide Survey*. New York: Basic Books, 1960.

Hadley, J. M. *Clinical and Counseling Psychology*. New York: Knopf, 1958.

Hall, Calvin S. and Lindzey, Gardner. *Theories of Personality*. New York: Wiley, 1957.

Harper, R. A. *Psychoanalysis and Psychotherapy: 36 Systems*. Englewood Cliffs, N.J.: Prentice-Hall, 1959.

Henry, A. F. and Short, J. E., Jr. *Suicide and Homicide*. Glencoe, Ill.: Free Press, 1954.

Heron, W. "The Pathology of Boredom," *Scientific American* (1957).

Hoff, E. C. "Alcoholism" in *The Encyclopedia of Mental Health*, ed. A. Deutsch and H. Fishman. Vol. 1. New York: Watts, 1963, pp. 179-204.

Hoffman, M. "Homosexual," *Psychology Today* 3 (July 1969): 43-45, 70.

Hollingshead, A. B. and Redlich, F. C. *Social Class and Mental Illness: A Community Study*. New York: Wiley, 1958.

Hurlock, Elizabeth B. *Adolescent Development*. 3d ed. New York: McGraw-Hill, 1967.

Hurst, L. A. "Genetic Factors" in *Handbook of Clinical Psychology*, ed. B. B. Wolman. New York: McGraw-Hill, 1965, pp. 141-80.

Jackson, J. K. "Alcoholism as a Family Crisis," *Pastoral Psychology* 13 (Apr. 1962): 8-18.

Janis, I. L. *Psychological Stress*. New York: Wiley, 1958.

Jellinek, E. M. "Phases in the Drinking History of Alcoholics: Analysis of a Survey Conducted by the *Grapevine*, Official Organ of Alcoholics Anonymous," *Quarterly Journal of Studies on Alcohol* (1946).

– – –. "Phases of Alcohol Addiction," *Quarterly Journal of Studies on Alcohol* 13 (1952): 673-78.

Jennings, G. J. "Drug Use and American Culture" in *Our Society in Turmoil*, ed. G. R. Collins. Carol Stream, Ill.: Creation House, 1970, pp. 81-97.

Joint Commission on Mental Illness and Health. *Action for Mental Health: Final Report of the Joint Commission on Mental Illness and Health*. New York: Science Editions, 1961.

Jones, H. K. *Toward a Christian Understanding of the Homosexual*. New York: Association, 1966.

Kahn, A. J. "Juvenile Delinquency" in *The Encyclopedia of Mental Health*, ed. A. Deutsch and H. Fishman. New York: Watts, 1963, pp. 893-907.

Keys, A.; Brozek, J.; Henschel, A.; Mickelson, O. and Taylor, H. L. *The Biology of Human Starvation*. Minneapolis: U. Minnesota, 1950.

Kaplan, B., ed. *The Inner World of Mental Illness*. New York: Harper & Row, 1964.

202

Kinsey, A. C.; Pomeroy, W. B. and Martin, C. E. "Concepts of Normality and Abnormality in Sexual Behavior" in *Psychosexual Development in Health and Disease*, ed. P H. Hoch and J. Zubin. New York: Grune & Stratton, 1949, pp. 11-32.

Kisker, G. W. *The Disorganized Personality.* New York: McGraw-Hill, 1964.

Knight, J. A. "The Use and Misuse of Religion by the Emotional Disturbed," *Pastoral Psychology* 13 (1962): 10-18.

Kubzansky, P. E. "The Effects of Reduced Environmental Stimulation on Human Behavior: A Review" in *The Manipulation of Human Behavior*, ed. A. D. Biderman and H. Zimmer. New York: Wiley, 1961, pp. 51-95.

Kullman, F. J. *Heredity in Health and Mental Disorder.* New York: Norton, 1953.

Kutash, S. B. "Psychoneuroses" in *Handbook of Clinical Psychology*, ed. B. B. Wolman. New York: McGraw-Hill, 1965, pp. 948-75.

Langner, T. S. and Michael, S. T. *Life Stress and Mental Health.* New York: Free Press of Glencoe, 1963.

Lazarus, A. *Behavior Therapy and Beyond.* New York: McGraw-Hill, 1971.

Leuba, C. "Toward Some Integration of Learning Theories: The Concept of Optimal Stimulation," *Psychological Reports* 1 (1955): 27-33.

Lombardi, D. N. "The Special Language of the Addict," *Pastoral Psychology* 20 (June 1969): 51-52.

Long, L. H., ed. *The World Almanac and Book of Facts.* (1970 edition) New York: Doubleday, 1969.

Lorand, S. and Balint, M., eds. *Perversions: Psychodynamics and Therapy.* New York: Random House, 1956.

Lord, W. *A Night to Remember.* New York: Holt, 1955.

Lowe, C. M. "Value Orientations—An Ethical Dilemma," *American Psychologist* 14 (1959): 687-93.

Lum, D. "The Church and the Prevention of Alcoholism," *Journal of Religion and Health* 9 (Apr. 1970): 138-61.

Maher, B. A. *Principles of Psychopathology: An Experimental Approach.* New York: McGraw-Hill, 1966.

Marcucci, R. "The Medical Aspects of Drug Abuse." Paper read at St. Mark's Reformed Episcopal Church, Jenkintown, Pa. (Apr. 26, 1969).

Masserman, J. H. *Modern Therapy of Personality Disorders.* Dubuque, Ia.: Brown, 1966.

Matarazzo, J. D. "The Interview" in *Handbook of Clinical Psychology*, ed. B. B. Wolman. New York: McGraw-Hill, 1965, pp. 403-50.

McNeil, E. B. *The Quiet Furies: Man and Disorder.* Englewood Cliffs, N. J.: Prentice-Hall, 1967.

Menninger, K.; Mayman, M. and Pruyser, P. *The Vital Balance.* New York: Viking, 1963.

Mensh, I. N. "Psychopathic Condition, Addictions, and Sexual Deviations" in *Handbook of Clinical Psychology*, ed. B. B. Wolman. New York: McGraw-Hill, 1965, pp. 1058-81.

Mintz, E. E. *Marathon Groups: Reality and Symbol.* New York: Appleton-Century-Crofts, 1971.

Montagu, A. "Chromosomes and Crime," *Psychology Today* 2 (October, 1968): pp. 43-49.

Mooney, R. L. *Mooney Problem Check List.* 1950 rcv. ed. New York: Psychological Corp., 1950.

Mowrer, O. H. *The Crisis in Psychiatry and Religion.* New York: Van Nostrand, 1961.

―――. *Morality and Mental Health.* Chicago: Rand McNally, 1967.

―――. "What Is Normal Behavior?" in *Introduction to Clinical Psychology,* ed. E. A. Berg and L. A. Pennington. 2d ed. New York: Ronald, 1954, pp. 58-88.

Mussen, P. H.; Conger, J. J. and Kagan, J. *Child Development and Personality.* 3d ed. New York: Harper & Row, 1969.

Naitoh, P. *Sleep Loss and Its Effect on Performance.* Dept. of the Navy, Bureau of Medicine and Surgery, Report no. 68-3 (Aug. 1969).

Nelson, M. H. *Why Christians Crack Up.* 2d ed. Chicago: Moody, 1968.

Noyes, A. P. and Kolb, L. C. *Modern Clinical Psychiatry.* 5th ed. Philadelphia: Saunders, 1958.

Oates, W. E. *When Religion Gets Sick.* Philadelphia: Westminster, 1970.

Page, J. D. *Psychopathology. The Science of Understanding Deviance.* Chicago: Aldine, 1971.

Patterson, C. H. "The Place of Values in Counseling and Psychotherapy," *Journal of Counseling Psychology* 5 (1958): 216-23.

Pattison, E. M. "Functions of the Clergy in Community Mental Health Centers," *Pastoral Psychology* 16 (1965): 21-26.

Peterson, E. *Psychopharmacology.* Dubuque, Ia.: Brown, 1966.

Pretzel, P. W. "The Role of the Clergyman in Suicide Prevention," *Pastoral Psychology* 21 (Apr. 1970): 47-52.

Pronko, N. H. *Textbook of Abnormal Psychology.* Baltimore: Williams & Wilkins, 1963.

Ramsey, G. W. "Aids for the Minister in Detecting Early Maladjustment," *Pastoral Psychology* 14 (Feb. 1963): 41-5.

Ridenour, F. *It All Depends.* Glendale, Calif.: Regal Books, 1969.

Rogers, C. R. *Client-Centered Therapy.* Boston: Houghton Mifflin, 1951.

Rosen, E. and Gregory, I. *Abnormal Psychology.* Philadelphia: Saunders, 1965.

Rosenthal, D. *Genetics of Psychopathology.* New York: McGraw-Hill, 1971.

Russell, B. *Why I Am Not a Christian: And Other Essays on Religion and Related Subjects.* New York: Simon & Schuster, 1957.

Sahakian, W. S., ed. *Psychopathology Today: Experimentation, Theory and Research.* Itasca, Ill.: Peacock, 1970.

Sargant, W. *Battle for the Mind: A Physiology of Conversion and and Brain Washing.* London: Pan Books, 1957.

Sauer, E. *In the Arena of Faith.* Grand Rapids: Eerdmans, 1955.

Sheldon, W. H. *The Varieties of Temperament: A Psychology of Con-*

*stitutional Differences.* New York: Harper, 1942.

Sherman, M. and Henry, T. R. *Hollow Folk.* New York: Crowell, 1933.

Shipp, T. J. *Helping the Alcoholic and His Family.* Philadelphia: Fortress, 1963.

Shneidman, E. S.; Farberow, N. L. and Litman, R. E. *The Psychology of Suicide.* New York: Science House, 1970.

Simon, W. "Sex," *Psychology Today* 3 (July 1968): 23-27.

Skinner, B. F. *The Technology of Teaching.* New York: Appleton-Century-Crofts, 1968.

Skinner, Tom. *Black and Free.* Grand Rapids: Zondervan, 1968.

Solomon, P.; Kusmansky, P. E.; Leiderman, P. H.; Mendelson, J. H.; Trumbull, R. and Wexler, D., eds. *Sensory Deprivation.* Cambridge: Harvard U., 1961.

Spock, B. "Psychology Can't Substitute for Morality" in *Morality and Mental Health,* ed. O. H. Mowrer. Chicago: Rand McNally, 1967, pp. 41-43.

Srole, L.; Langner, T. S.; Michael, S. C.; Opler, M. K. and Rennie, P. A. C. *Mental Health in the Metropolis: The Midtown Manhattan Study.* Vol. 1. New York: McGraw-Hill, 1962.

St. Clair, R. J. *Neurotics in the Church.* Westwood, N. J.: Revell, 1963.

Stierlin, H. "Psychoses" in *The Encyclopedia of Mental Health,* ed. A. Deutsch and H. Fishmann. Vol. 5. New York: Watts, 1963, pp. 1664-77.

Strange, J. R. *Abnormal Psychology: Understanding Behavior Disorders.* New York: McGraw-Hill, 1965.

Symonds, P. M. *The Psychology of Parent-Child Relationships.* New York: Appleton-Century, 1939.

Szasz, T. S. "The Myth of Mental Illness," *American Psychologist* 15 (1960): 113-18.

"Technical Recommendations for Psychological Tests and Diagnostic Techniques," *Psychological Bulletin* 51 (1954). Supplement.

Terman, L. M. and Oden, M. H. *The Gifted Group at Mid-Life.* Vol. 5 in *Genetic Studies of Genius.* Stanford, Calif.: Stanford U., 1959.

Thrope, L. P.; Katz, B. and Lewis, R. T. *The Psychology of Abnormal Behavior.* 2d ed. New York: Ronald, 1961.

Toffler, A. *Future Shock.* New York: Random House, 1970.

Trew, A. "The Religious Factor in Mental Illness," *Pastoral Psychology* 22 (May 1971): 21-28.

Trouton, D. and Eysenck, H. J. "The Effects of Drugs on Behavior" in *Handbook of Abnormal Psychology: An Experimental Approach,* ed. H. J. Eysenck. New York: Basic Books, 1961, pp. 634-96.

Tweedie, D. F. *The Christian and the Couch: An Introduction to Christian Logotherapy.* Grand Rapids: Baker, 1963.

Tyler, L. E. *Tests and Measurements.* 2d ed. Englewood Cliffs, N. J.: Prentice-Hall, 1971.

Vincent, M. O. "Suicide and How to Prevent It," *Christianity Today* 14 (Jan. 16, 1970): 10-12.

Watkins, J. G. "Psychotherapeutic Methods" in *Handbook of Clinical Psychology,* ed. B. B. Wolman. New York: McGraw-Hill, 1965, pp. 1143-67.

Weatherhead, L. D. *Psychology, Religion and Healing.* London: Hodder & Stoughton, 1951.

*Webster's New Collegiate Dictionary.* Springfield, Mass.: Merriam, 1961.

Weisskopf-Joelson, Edith. "Logotherapy and Existential Analysis," *Acta Psychotherapeutica* (1958): 193-304.

West, D. J. *Homosexuality.* Harmondsworth, Middlesex, England: Penguin Books, 1960.

Wilkerson, D. *The Cross and the Switchblade.* Old Tappan, N. J.: Revell, 1962.

Wolman, B. B. "Schizophrenia and Related Disorders" in *Handbook of Clinical Psychology.* New York: McGraw-Hill, 1965, pp. 976-1029.

Yablonsky, L. *Synanon: The Tunnel Back.* Baltimore: Penguin Books, 1965.

Zax, M. and Stricker, G. *Patterns of Psychopathology: Case Studies of Behavioral Dysfunction.* New York: Macmillan, 1963.

# INDEX

## A

abnormal behavior 9, 10-12, 14, 17, 23, 78-82, 93, 101, 177
  causes 10, 13-51, 79, 83, 84, 114, 118-9
  definition 10-12
  reactions 113-157
accidents 15, 22, 23, 34, 38, 50, 51, 136, 150, 152, 163
acne 148
addiction 10, 159
adjustment 35, 40, 46, 70, 73, 79, 81, 105, 142, 149, 153, 154,
  155, 157
adultery 184
affective disorders 75, 115, 119-21
aggression 38, 43, 71, 77, 78, 118, 127, 143, 170
alcohol, alcoholism 59, 66, 73, 77, 114, 159-69, 171, 175, 191
  causes 163-64
  development 161, 163
  iocal church and, 167-68
  prevention 168-69
  treatment 165
Alcoholics Anonymous 165, 166, 167, 168, 175
American Psychiatric Association 116, 148
American Psychological Association 110
anger 18, 141
anthropologists 40
antidepressants 101, 102, 173
antisocial personality 77, 185-86
anxiety, anxious 11, 23, 25, 27, 34, 36, 37, 38, 39, 50, 56, 62,
  63, 64, 70, 71, 75, 76, 78, 95, 101, 122, 123, 124, 125, 126,
  127, 128, 129, 130, 133, 134, 135, 139, 140, 143, 147, 148,
  151, 152, 153, 155, 156, 157, 164, 174

208

# G

gastrointestinal disorders 148
genius 80, 82
glands 15, 33-34, 73
goals 11, 51, 103, 109, 121
God 11, 12, 24, 25, 27, 29, 43, 48, 49, 57, 62, 67, 69, 70, 79, 103, 107, 131, 134, 141, 165, 166, 167, 177, 180, 183, 184, 189, 191, 192
Graham, Billy 122, 140
Graham-Kendall Memory for Designs Test 98, 99
group 21, 40, 43, 46, 106, 157, 170
group therapy 104, 105-06, 111
guilt 15, 27-29, 37, 43, 51, 68, 71, 75, 82, 101, 122, 127, 134, 136, 137, 139, 143, 147, 152, 153, 167, 179, 184, 186

# H

hallucinations 17, 27, 59, 71, 73, 74, 116, 117, 122, 123, 155, 156
happiness 10, 61
healing 130
health 34, 51, 63, 121, 136, 138, 148, 155
hell 49
heredity 15, 30-32, 51
Holland 177
Holy Spirit 29, 48, 62, 128, 134, 183
homosexuality 31, 77, 122, 177, 180, 182-83, 184
hospitals, mental 26, 27, 30, 43, 44, 55, 68, 72, 75, 79, 81, 82, 84, 87, 88, 99, 100, 106, 107, 111, 115, 154, 157, 159, 190
hostility 36, 37, 74, 118, 135, 136, 140, 147, 151, 157, 179, 188
hypnotherapy 106
hysterical personality 97

# I

illness 16, 56
illusion 59
immature personality 146
impotence 148
inadequate personality 77, 144-46
incest 180, 183
individual therapy 104-05, 111
inkblot test 95, 97
insecure, insecurity 11, 25, 27, 36, 37, 38, 39, 41, 42, 44, 49, 56, 70, 124, 125

P

pain 50, 56, 57, 58, 61, 137, 138, 153, 169, 179
panic 23, 76, 126, 147, 151
paranoid personality 76, 140-41
paranoid states 75, 115, 121-22
parents 24, 36, 38, 149, 155, 164, 168, 174, 184, 186, 188, 189
passive-aggressive personality 77, 143-44
pastors 9, 11, 28, 40, 99, 108, 121, 124, 126, 135, 139, 143, 152, 163, 183
Paul the Apostle 34, 38, 48, 62, 68, 131, 183
perception 15, 39, 40, 42, 50, 51, 57-60, 61, 68, 71, 76, 80, 82, 89, 103
performance tests 94
permissiveness 15, 35, 37
personality 17, 18, 76
personality disorders 76, 139-47, 158
phobias 60, 131-33
prayer 25, 49, 50, 70, 134, 139, 165, 166
precipitating factors 15, 16-29, 50, 51
predisposing factors 15, 29-50, 51
pressure 20, 22, 27, 39, 42, 48, 51, 107, 128, 138, 155, 159, 161, 170, 171
pride 61
prison 191
problems 14, 22, 70, 78, 79, 80, 81, 88, 101, 103, 105, 108, 111, 136, 139, 145, 146, 148, 155, 167, 168
projection 20
projective tests 94, 95-98
prostitution 177, 184
psychiatrist 14, 25, 41, 47, 55, 67, 78, 85-87, 91, 99, 100, 102, 108, 111, 126, 191
psychoanalysis 104
psychoanalyst 87, 111
psychologist 14, 25, 26, 29, 36, 40, 53, 67, 78, 84, 91, 94, 95, 95, 96, 98, 108, 110, 111, 126, 127, 130, 156, 177, 180, 191
psychopathic personality 31
psychophsiological disorders 79, 147-49, 158
psychosis 73, 74-75, 81, 115-22, 123, 157, 159
psychosomatic reactions 56, 148
psychosurgery 103
psychotherapy, see therapy
punishment 36

Q

questionnaires 15, 93, 98

214

# R

race 40, 44-45
rating scale 91, 92, 98
rebellion 36, 38, 171, 187
rejection 15, 35, 36, 39
religion 15, 25, 40, 42, 43, 46, 48, 49, 67, 68, 93, 108, 110,
    124, 133-34, 177
research 84, 85, 110, 111, 112, 118, 164, 171
respiratory disorders 148
retirement 155
rigidity 49, 125
Rogers, C. 105
Rorschach, H. 95, 97, 98
Russell, B. 49

# S

sadism 77, 179
Salvation Army 189
Schein, E. 156
schizoid personality 77, 141-42
schizophrenia 30, 32, 33, 74-75, 115-19
    catatonic 74, 117-18
    causes of 118-19
    hebephrenic 10, 72, 74, 113, 117
    other types 74-75, 118-19
    paranoid 74, 118, 121
    simple 74, 116-17
scripture 29, 38, 48, 69, 153, 168, 185
self-confidence 58
self-control 48
self-esteem 11, 23, 58, 122
self-identity 103
self-report technique 93, 94
sentence-completion tests 93
sex 15, 32, 40, 43, 45, 66, 159, 169, 171
sex deviation 10, 14, 77, 177-85
    categories of 178-81
    causes, treatment, prevention 181-82
    church and 182-85
Shakespeare 27, 33, 65
shame 61
Sheldon, W. 33
shock 23, 39, 45, 101, 107, 111, 120, 150, 151
sin 15, 25-27, 51, 70, 79, 82, 134, 163, 183, 189-91
Skinner, Tom 189

client-centered 104-05
drug 101, 111
group 105-06, 111, 165
individual 104-05, 111, 165
logotherapy 105, 107
milieu 106-07, 119
pschotherapy 48, 85, 103-06, 107, 108, 109-10, 119, 120, 121,
    144, 149, 182
  shock 101, 102, 111, 121, 135
  spiritual 107-08, 111
thinking 15, 17, 60-61, 68, 71, 74, 75, 80, 82, 95, 115, 122,
    156
Thomas 69
tranquilizers 101
transient situational disorders 78, 149-57, 158
transvestism 77, 179, 182
trauma 15, 38
treatment 79, 81, 82, 83, 84, 86, 100-08, 111, 112, 114, 148,
    149, 152, 154, 165, 167, 169, 175, 176
tumor 19
Tweedie, D. 107

U

ulcers 56, 77, 148
unconscious 65, 68, 75
underactivity 65, 71
unemployment 23
unhappiness 11, 62, 63, 70, 125
United States 16, 23, 34, 44, 45, 81, 84, 124, 160, 164, 178,
    187
urinalysis 15

V

Vaas, J. 189
values 24, 25, 48, 108, 109-10, 111, 170, 188
voyeurism 77, 179

W

war 15, 17, 19, 21, 22-23, 34, 46, 51, 66, 136, 152, 153, 154,
    157
Wechsler Adult Intelligence Scale (WAIS) 94-95
Wechsler Intelligence Scale for Children (WISC) 94
withdrawal 15, 20, 66, 71, 78, 116
worry 75, 121
worship 25, 39, 134

X

X-ray 15, 19

217